Student Book 3

Fully revised 4th edition

Your Life

The whole-school solution for PSHE and Citizenship

T0340550

John Foster and Simon Foster

Published by Collins
An imprint of HarperCollins*Publishers*
The News Building
1 London Bridge Street
London
SE1 9GF

HarperCollins *Publishers*
Macken House,
39/40 Mayor Street Upper,
Dublin 1,
D01 C9W8,
Ireland

Browse the complete Collins catalogue at
www.collins.co.uk

© HarperCollins*Publishers* Limited 2014

10

ISBN-13 978-0-00-759271-5

British Library Cataloguing in Publication Data
A Catalogue record for this publication is available from the British Library.

Commissioned by Letitia Luff

Managed by Caroline Green

Edited by Vicky Leech

Designed and typeset by Jordan Publishing Design Limited and eMC Design Ltd

Copy-edited by Donna Cole

Proofread by Cassie Fox and Lyn Miller

Indexed by Jane Henley

Cover design by Angela English

Cover photograph by Yanlev/Dreamstime

Production by Rachel Weaver

Printed and Bound in the UK by Ashford Colour Press Ltd.

Acknowledgments

The publishers wish to thank the following for permission to reproduce photographs. Every effort has been made to trace copyright holders and to obtain their permission for the use of copyright materials. The publishers will gladly receive any information enabling them to rectify any error or omission at the first opportunity.

(t = top, c = centre, b = bottom, r = right, l = left)

Cover Yanlev/Dreamstime, p6 Creatista/Shutterstock, p7 Blend Images/Shutterstock, p8 szefei/Shutterstock, p9 Jamie Wilson/Shutterstock, p10 Djomas/Shutterstock, p11 Clive Chilvers/Shutterstock, p12 VI-Images/Getty Images, p13 Zurijeta/Shutterstock, p14 WaveBreakMedia/Shutterstock, p15 Minerva Studio/Shutterstock, p16 MJTH/Shutterstock, p18tl Claudia Paulussen/Shutterstock, p18tr Monkey Business Images/Shutterstock, p18bl Antb/Shutterstock, p18br Fisherss/Shutterstock, p19 WaveBreakMedia/Shutterstock, p20 iLight Foto/Shutterstock, p21 Suzanne Tucker/Shutterstock, p22 Black Rock Digital/Shutterstock, p23 imtmphoto/Shutterstock, p24 Image Point Fr/Shutterstock, p25 Sirapob/Shutterstock, p26 Ron Sachs/CNP/Corbis, p27 Bloomberg/Getty Images, p28 Oleg Zabielin/Shutterstock, p29 Asianet-Pakistan/Shutterstock, p30 WaveBreakMedia/Shutterstock, p31 Pixelbliss/Shutterstock, p32 Pogonici/Shutterstock, p33t Pressmaster/Shutterstock, p33b KenDrysdale/Shutterstock, p34 Sabphoto/Shutterstock, p35t Radiokafka/Shutterstock, p35b Locrifa/Shutterstock, p36 EJWhite/Shutterstock, p37 Peter Bernik/Shutterstock, p38 Againstar/Shutterstock, p39 Photographee.eu/Shutterstock, p40 Piotr Marcinski/Shutterstock, p42 Philippe Turpin/Photononstop/Corbis, p43 Valerie Potapova/Shutterstock, p44 Maxriesgo/Shutterstock, p45 Fotoluminate LLC/Shutterstock, p47 Pressmaster/Shutterstock, p48 Alessandro Colle/Shutterstock, p50 Creatista/Shutterstock, p51 Photographee.eu/Shutterstock, p52l Djem/Shutterstock, p52r EduardSV/Shutterstock, p53t Jeh_Somwang/Shutterstock, p53ct Blablo101/Shutterstock, p53cb BlueRingMedia/Shutterstock, p53b GlOck/Shutterstock, p54 Minerva Studio/Shutterstock, p55 Mangostock/Shutterstock, p56 Astrelok/Shutterstock, p57 Syda Productions/Shutterstock, p58r Featureflash/Shutterstock, p58tl Helga Esteb/Shutterstock, p58bl Featureflash/Shutterstock, p59 Black Rock Digital/Shutterstock, p60 Barcroft Media/Getty Images, p61 Barcroft Media/Getty Images, p62 Tibanna79/Shutterstock, p63 George Pimentel/IMG/Getty Images, p64 Tyler Olson/Shutterstock, p65 WaveBreakMedia/Shutterstock, p66 oliveromg/Shutterstock, p68 Michael Jung/Shutterstock, p69 Monkey Business Images/Shutterstock, p70 sakhorn/Shutterstock, p71 BrAt82/Shutterstock, p72 Lenka Kozuchova/Shutterstock, p73 BasPhoto/Shutterstock, p74l Natalia Sheinkin/Shutterstock, p74r Elzbieta Sekowska/Shutterstock, p76 Christopher Furlong/Getty Images, p77 Vic and Julie Pigula/Shutterstock, p78 Khakimullin Aleksandr/Shutterstock, p79t Photographee.eu/Shutterstock, p79b Sebastian Kaulitzki/Shutterstock, p81 Sebastian Kaulitzki/Shutterstock, p82 Bikeworldtravel/Shutterstock, p83 Happystock/Shutterstock, p84 Mangostock/Shutterstock, p85 Nenetus/Shutterstock, p87 Flip Nicklin/Minden Pictures/Corbis, p88 Ken Wolter/Shutterstock, p90 Ermolaev Alexander/Shutterstock, p92 Nobor/Shutterstock, p93 UbjsP/Shutterstock, p95 Specnaz/Shutterstock, p96 Migel/Shutterstock, p97t Dieter Hawlan/Shutterstock, p97b Cooperr/Shutterstock, p98 William Perugini/Shutterstock, p99 Michaelpuche/Shutterstock, p100 WaveBreakMedia/Shutterstock, p101 LeviQ/Shutterstock, p102 AFH/Shutterstock, p103 Piotr Marcinski/Shutterstock, p104 Agsandrew/Shutterstock, p105 Mikael Damkier/Shutterstock, p106 Anton_Ivanov/Shutterstock, p107 Charles Harker/Shutterstock, p108 ESTUDI M6/Shutterstock, p109 Photosani/Shutterstock.

Contents

Introducing *Your Life*

Your Life Student Book 3 is the third of three books which together form a comprehensive course in Personal, Social and Health Education (PSHE) and Citizenship at Key Stage 3. The table shows how the topics covered in this book meet requirements of the National Curriculum for Citizenship at Key Stage 3 and provide a coherent course in PSHE for students in Year 9.

Personal, Social and Health Education

Personal wellbeing – Understanding yourself and handling relationships	Social education – Responsibilities and values	Keeping healthy
These units concentrate on developing your self-knowledge and your ability to manage your emotions and how to handle relationships.	These units concentrate on exploring social issues and on developing an understanding of your responsibilities towards other people in society, your values and your opinions.	These units are designed to help you take care of your physical and mental health.
• **You and your feelings** – dealing with loss	• **You and your responsibilities** – racism, prejudice and discrimination	• **You and your body** – adolescence
• **You and your decisions** – how to make decisions	• **You and the media** – the power of the press	• **You and your body** – safe sex, STIs and AIDS
• **You and your family** – becoming an adult	• **You and other people** – people with mental illnesses	• **You and your safety** – eating disorders
• **You an other people** – being assertive		• **You and your body** – drugs and drugtaking
• **You and your achievements** – reviewing your progress		

The various activities within each unit provide opportunities for you to learn how to grow as individuals, for example, by developing self-awareness and taking responsibility for keeping healthy and handling your money. The group discussion activities involve you in learning how to work as a team and how to develop the skills of co-operation and negotiation. You are presented with situations in which you have to work with others, to analyse information, to consider moral and social dilemmas and to make choices and decisions.

Citizenship

Becoming an active citizen

These units focus on the society in which you live, on its laws and government and on developing the skills you require to become an active citizen.

- **You and the law**
  – crimes and punishment

- **You as a citizen**
  – political parties

- **You and your values**
  – civil liberties and human rights

- **You and the law**
  – the justice system

- **You and global issues**
  – poverty

- **You and the community**
  – pressure groups and campaigning

Economic and financial capability

These units aim to help you to manage your money effectively, to learn about the world of work and to practise the skills of being enterprising.

- **You and your money**
  – banking and ways of saving

- **You and the media**
  – you as a consumer

- **You and the world of work**
  – investigating careers

- **You and the world of work**
  – your choices

Your identity and image

Your teenage years are a period of rapid growth and change known as adolescence, during which you develop from a child into an adult. Your body changes and you develop sexually as you pass through puberty. Your character also changes. You become more independent, developing a greater sense of your identity and your own views, values and beliefs.

You and your identity

An important aspect of your identity is your personality – the features of your character that make you the sort of person you are.

What type of person are you? Do you see yourself as quiet and reserved or lively and outgoing? Are you anxious or carefree? Do you enjoy being with other people or do you prefer being on your own?

Thinking about questions like these can help you to discover what sort of personality you have and to establish your identity.

In groups

What characteristics would your ideal person have? On your own, study the list of characteristics right. Rank them in order of importance, starting with 1 (the most important). Then form groups and discuss your lists.

humble loyal practical reliable

confident gentle intelligen

generous

artistic hard-working

honest **considerate**

sociable *attractive* witty athletic

wealthy exciting forgiving **tough**

Your goals and ambitions

During adolescence, you may start to think about what you want to do with your life and what you hope to achieve. At first you may have no firm ideas about what you want to do. This may only become clear to you over a number of years, and you may change your mind many times before making a decision. Nevertheless, thinking about what you hope to achieve can be a useful way of developing your sense of identity.

In 10 years' time

Here's what some people said when they were asked to think about what they'd like to have achieved in 10 years' time:

"I'd like to have travelled and seen the world."

"I want to be rich and famous."

"I'd like to have got a university degree and found an interesting job."

"I want to have had a good time. After all, you're only young once."

"I'd like to have done something to help other people who are less fortunate than us."

For your file

Write about how you see yourself in 10 years' time and what you hope to have achieved by then.

You and your image

The impression of yourself you give to others depends chiefly on two things – the way you behave and the way you look.

There are lots of pressures on teenagers to make them dress or behave in certain ways; from parents, teachers and other teenagers; and from advertisers, television, newspapers and magazines. When you're deciding how you're going to behave and how you want to look, you need to be aware of these pressures.

In groups

Discuss the advice Jane Goldman gives (below) about the importance of being yourself and dressing the way you want to. Do you agree that 'most people want friends who are happy, balanced and behave normally'?

Discuss the advice she gives about how to cope with fashion. Do you agree that 'real friends don't care what you wear'? How important do you think it is to dress fashionably?

Give the right impression – *be yourself*

Are you boastful?

Showing off and doing things that demand attention rarely wins any friends. It not only gives the impression that you're trying too hard, but it's also unattractive behaviour, and likely to put people off wanting to get to know you better. Being yourself is always the best bet.

Are you ultra-nice?

Being friendly wins points, but being 'creepy' doesn't. If you constantly agree with things people say, regularly compliment them on their clothes, talents etc, then you are being crawly and it's very off-putting. Most people want friends who are happy and balanced.

Do you dress differently from others?

Sadly, many young people are suspicious of others who don't conform. Whether it's because of your religion, because you're not into fashion, or simply because you like to be individual, just the fact that you stand out can put people off you. However, you should never need to change the way you look to suit others – just make an extra effort to get talking to people, show them that you *like* the way *they* are, and once they've got to know your personality, they'll place much less emphasis on how you look.

Four ways to cope with fashion

1 If something comes into fashion, it's never worth pestering for it or breaking your piggy bank right away unless you truly adore it and could imagine yourself wearing it even *after* it went out of fashion. Wait a few weeks, and if you still want it, then it's probably worth it.

3 Never be afraid to avoid a fad you're not that crazy about, even if all your friends are doing it. If you don't like it and it doesn't suit you, leave it. Real friends don't care what you wear.

2 If there's no chance of getting anything new for a while, but you feel like your clothes are embarrassingly out of date, your best bet is to wear stuff that's either classic (like jeans and a sweatshirt) or totally off-beat, because it makes a positive statement that you're *aware* of fashion but have deliberately chosen not to follow it.

4 Don't get too hung up about fashion – there really are far more important things in life. If your friends disagree with this statement, it's worth seriously considering getting some new, less shallow ones.

Dealing with your feelings

Mood swings

Do you sometimes feel happy one minute and sad the next? These sudden changes of mood are a very normal part of growing up. Some of the problems might be caused by your hormones, which are responsible for the physical changes you are going through.

You are changing from a child into a young adult, and new experiences are changing your view of the world. You may be excited and stimulated by what you discover. But you may also feel moody because you no longer enjoy the same things that you used to.

It's easy to blame the people around you for your state of mind. Perhaps you're feeling frustrated with your parents because they just don't seem to understand you any more. You may feel differently about your friends too. Some childhood friends now seem juvenile and annoying. Your mood can swing from wildly happy to desperately sad and back again.

Someone to talk to

Have you heard the saying 'a problem shared is a problem halved'? If you keep your problems to yourself they can seem a great deal worse than they really are. If you talk to somebody about your problem, you can come to see it in a different light. Maybe it's just arranging an emotion into words and then saying it out loud that does this. Sometimes you will find that the person you talk to can convince you that there is really nothing to worry about at all.

Different people can help you with different problems so, if you want to share a worry, decide who would be the best person to talk to about it.

In groups

Study the list of problems (below) and decide which of these people you think it would be best to consult about that particular problem: **a)** best friend, **b)** parent, **c)** elder sibling/ sibling, **d)** teacher, **e)** agony aunt, **f)** doctor, **g)** religious leader, **h)** social worker, **i)** confidential adviser, for example Childline.

1 Worries about your physical development or a sexual problem.

2 Constant arguments with your parents.

3 An emotional problem related to your boyfriend/girlfriend.

4 Unhappiness because you are being teased or bullied.

5 A problem because you have got involved in something illegal.

6 Loneliness because you don't seem able to make or keep friends.

Anger   Difficult

"I get so angry all the time. My mum says I've got a problem and that I have to learn to calm down. But no matter how hard I try, something happens and I explode." Cara

Anger is one of the primary emotions, and despite its reputation it isn't a bad emotion. Like joy, pain and happiness, anger is a natural response to certain events. And just as expressing your happiness makes you feel good, it's better to express your anger rather than bottle it up where it ferments into nastiness.

Okay, so we agree that it's good to express your anger, the trouble comes when you act on your anger by taking it out on others or yourself. Look at exactly why you lash out and what you hope to achieve when you do. Rather than hit out or have a door-slamming session, count to ten, have a quiet think, and work out an assertive plan of action.

Coping with your moods

Although you can't avoid bad moods altogether, there are ways of controlling them. First of all, don't blame yourself for being moody. Try to think back over the hours until you hit on the moment things went wrong. The reason behind your mood swing may surprise you.

For example, one afternoon somebody takes your seat on the school bus. This makes you angry and upset, although it's nothing very serious. Your friends think you're silly for getting upset about it and when you think about it seriously afterwards, you will probably admit that losing your seat wasn't the real problem at all. Perhaps it simply triggered off all kinds of other thoughts about yourself. You think it shows that nobody likes you, or that people take you for granted. It's really these feelings that are at the core of your reaction.

Think positive

Finding the reason behind your bad moods should help you do something about them. Learn to recognize moods and control them, or they might start controlling you.

Positive action of some kind will make you feel better.

If you feel moody, take some time to be by yourself. Go for a walk or do something physical like a bike ride. When you've thought things over, you may be ready to talk to somebody. Doing something physical rather than mental for a while may make all the difference.

If there are certain people or situations that put you into a bad mood, try to avoid them. It is worth telling people how you feel if you would rather be left alone. It can be unhelpful if people try to make you have a good time when you don't feel like it.

Discuss what you have learned from these two pages about **a)** mood swings and how to cope with them, and **b)** how to deal with anger and frustration. Which pieces of advice do you think are the most useful?

For your file

**Dear Dave
I'm finding life hard at present. Some days I feel great and everything's fine, other days I'm really down and people get on to me for being moody. Is there anything I can do to stop myself feeling like this?**
Aston (14)

Write Dave's reply to Aston.

Feelings   Frustration

"Sometimes I feel so frustrated that I could scream. I feel like I'm trapped and that no-one can hear what I'm saying." Lena

Feeling frustrated comes from being misunderstood, ignored, or from being unable to achieve desired goals. Often a sense of frustration comes about because we don't really know what our goals are, so we thrash about trying different things only to find we're still not satisfied.

To give frustration its marching orders you have to accept that long-term happiness comes from within, and not from boyfriends or girlfriends, new clothes, the latest phone, careers, money or from going out. If you work at getting to know yourself (and liking what you find), then you won't look elsewhere for happiness.

Racism and racists

What is racism?

Racism is the belief that people of some races are inferior or superior to others, judging by things like the colour of their skin, their ethnic origin or the country they come from.

Prejudice is knowing little about people but forming an opinion on them anyway on the basis of stereotypes.

Racial discrimination occurs when someone is treated less well because of their skin colour or their racial, national or ethnic origin. Racial discrimination includes racial abuse and harassment and is against the law.

In pairs

What is the difference between racism, prejudice and racial discrimination?

Racism is...

Five teenagers explain what racism means to them.

Having to keep relationships secret

"I can't walk down the street with my boyfriend because our families wouldn't approve of us going out together." *Lisa, 15*

Being ignored

"I'm Jewish so I didn't have to sing the hymns at assembly. I thought that was reasonable until the other girls at school started to ignore me because one said I thought I was something special." *Hannah, 13*

Being singled out

"I was in McDonald's and these lads said to my friend, 'Why are you going round with a Paki?' and pointed at me. Then they made jokes about there being a smell of curry." *Parveen, 17*

Ignorance at home

"My mum says she doesn't mind me having friends who are black, but she would draw the line at me going out with 'one of them'." *Karl, 15*

Not getting the respect you deserve

"I hate the way people talk to me as though I can't speak English, just because my parents are Chinese. They own a restaurant and you would not believe the abuse they have to endure." *Anna, 18*

In groups

1 Discuss what the five teenagers (above) say racism means to them and how it affects them. Talk about what racism means to you.

2 'Racist jokes such as the ones made to Parveen aren't funny. As well as being insulting, they demean the person who tells them.' Discuss this view.

Why are some people racist?

Racism is defined as thought or action based on the belief that some of the 'races of mankind' are superior to others.

Historically, the 'superior races' were seen as more civilised, intelligent and more capable of scientific invention and moral behaviour. This idea of 'higher races' and 'lower races' has been used to justify slavery, forced transportation, economic exploitation and even genocide – the killing of hundreds of thousands of men, women and children – because they were said to be members of certain 'races' and should be controlled or eliminated.

Not only has this cruel thinking inflicted enormous human suffering, the idea it is based on – that there are distinct, ordered racial categories – is now known by genetic science to be incorrect. Nonetheless, racism is still prevalent today.

Within the human form, the range of differences is very large, and the clustering of features such as skin colour and hair type – which are often taken to be the signs of racial difference – are just a tiny part of the possible range of DNA variation of which we are made up. People with similar skin colour, for example, though alike in that way, are genetically unalike in so many other ways that to say they are members of a distinct 'race' makes little more sense than to say that people who can roll their tongues longways, and those who can't, are two distinct 'races'!

In groups

1. 'There is only one race – the human race.' What does this mean?

2. Discuss how the idea that there are superior 'races' has been used in the past to justify slavery, the persecution of the Jews in Nazi Germany and the system of apartheid in South Africa. Talk about the suffering that resulted.

In groups

Discuss the reasons which are suggested on this page as to why people are racist. Can you think of any other reasons? What do you think is the main reason?

Racists
what's their problem?

Present-day racists hold their views for a number of different reasons …

Insecurity: Racist people might not feel very good about themselves, so by bullying others they can feel powerful.

Upbringing: Many have racist views because their parents hold the same, misguided beliefs.

Bad experiences: Perhaps they've been in a situation before that has made them dislike an individual with different colour skin. They may now hate people from the same background.

Fear of the unknown: Racists are afraid of uncertainties – they despise what they don't understand and have no interest in learning about other cultures or nationalities.

Arrogance: They believe that if everyone had the same upbringing and opinions as them the world would be perfect.

Intolerance: Racists believe people of other colours or nationalities to their own shouldn't be living in their country.

11

How great a problem is racism?

Racism can make it harder for people to get jobs, or keep their jobs; it can mean they have poorer housing, or that they leave school or college with fewer qualifications; it can result in violent attacks, or it can lead to harsh treatment by the police or other authorities.

- Historically, unemployment among ethnic minority groups has been around double that of white people.
- According to the UK 2011 census, black and minority ethnic (BME) households are more than twice as likely to be homeless as white households.

Racism in park football

In March 2012 a group of Bangladeshi children playing football in Dagenham were racially abused by a large number of spectators. Nine arrests were made.

'I coach park football every week and I see racial abuse consistently.' *Colin King, Black and Asian Coaches Association*.

How serious a problem do you think racism is in park football? Should referees stop park matches if spectators make racist comments? Should abusive and violent parents be given red cards?

Racism in football

Racism in football remains a problem, despite the efforts of the *Kick It Out* campaign.

- In 2012 Serbian fans made racist chants at England under 21 international Danny Rose, during a European Championship match. The Serbian FA was fined £65 000.

- In 2012, Liverpool's Luis Suarez was banned for 8 matches for racially abusing Manchester United's Patrice Evra.

- Dynamo Kiev were ordered to play their next two European matches in empty stadiums because their fans racially abused players from Paris St Germaine and Bordeaux.

- A match in Italy was abandoned when AC Milan's Kevin Prince-Boateng walked off the pitch after being racially abused.

- Chelsea's John Terry was banned for 4 matches and fined £220 000 for making a racist remark to Queen's Park Rangers' Anton Ferdinand.

In groups

Discuss what you learn from the stories on this page about what it feels like to be a victim of racism.

Role play

In pairs, imagine that one of you has been the victim of racial harassment or racial abuse. Act out a scene in which someone tells a friend what happened and how they felt during the incident and afterwards. Do the scene twice, taking it in turns to be the person who has been the victim of racism.

In groups

1 Are the punishments handed out for racist behaviour at football matches too lenient?

2 Should players who make racist comments be banned for at least six months?

3 Should clubs whose supporters make racist comments be docked points or thrown out of cup competitions?

4 Should referees abandon matches when racist chanting occurs?

5 Should teams whose supporters make racist chants have their stadiums closed and be forced to play several matches at neutral grounds from which travelling fans are banned?

6 Draw up a five-point plan to stamp out racism in football.

How much discrimination is there?

Islamophobia is the fear and/or hatred of Muslims and Islamic culture, in the belief that all Muslims are religious fanatics.

Tell Mama is a project backed by the government to record anti-Muslim hate incidents. Mama stands for Measuring Anti-Muslim Attacks. In its first year it recorded 632 incidents, three-quarters of which consisted of online abuse.

Other incidents involved verbal abuse of people wearing Islamic clothing, smashing the windows of mosques and direct attempts to offend Muslims. For example, in December 2012, a cross wrapped in ham was left outside the home of the family of Murad Alam in Bingham, Nottinghamshire.

Mr Alam said: 'To be honest I don't think Islamophobia is taken very seriously – if what happened to me happened to a Jewish family there would have been outrage.'

Muslims under siege

A report on Islamophobia published in 2008 investigated the scale and depth of prejudice against Muslims in Britain. It concluded that the deep resentment and fear of British Muslims after the 11 September and 7 July terrorist attacks has shown itself in increased racial abuse and violent attacks on innocent people.

The prejudice against Muslims has been expressed in many different forms, but the most prevalent has been the attack from the media where the Muslim community has faced particularly hostile coverage.

A team of researchers studied coverage of Islam over 8 years. It was found that almost two-thirds of the stories were about terrorism;

22% were about religious issues such as Sharia law, and approximately 8% about extremism relating to figures like Abu Hamza. Almost all the reports portrayed Muslims as a source of trouble. Only 5% of stories were based on problems facing British Muslims.

In groups

How serious a problem do you think Islamophobia is? Is there less outrage at anti-Muslim incidents than anti-Semitic incidents?

Is media coverage of the Muslim community prejudiced?

While condemning Islamophobic attitudes and behaviour, the journalist Polly Toynbee says: 'Muslims must respect the right of others to criticise religions without smearing any critic as racist.' Discuss this view.

What is institutional racism?

"The collective failure of an organisation to provide an appropriate and professional service to people because of their colour, culture or ethnic origin." – The Macpherson Report

"Institutional racism is about stereotyping; it is about being unwitting; it is about ignorance; it is about failing to recognise a racist/hate crime; it is about not listening or understanding and not being interested in listening or understanding; it is about white pretence and black people being seen as a problem." – John Grieve, former director of the Metropolitan Police's Racial Task Force

In groups

What is racial discrimination? Which groups of people are the main victims of racial discrimination? How serious a problem do you think racial discrimination is in Britain today? Is media coverage of the Muslim community prejudiced?

In groups

Discuss what is meant by institutional racism and its effects.

Racism and the law

Racial discrimination and the law

The Race Relations Act (1976) made racial discrimination unlawful:

- in employment
- in education
- in the provision of goods and services, whether by individuals, businesses or local authorities
- in the sale, purchase and management of property.

The Act defined two types of discrimination – direct discrimination and indirect discrimination. Direct discrimination occurs in a situation where a person is treated less favourably than another person would be on racial grounds. Indirect discrimination occurs where there is a rule, policy, practice or condition that is applied to everyone equally but in practice leads to unequal treatment of people of one racial or ethnic group.

Although the Act prohibited both types of discrimination, indirect discrimination was outlawed only in limited respects in the public sector. Therefore, in 2000 Parliament introduced another Race Relations Act that extended the law to make indirect discrimination unlawful throughout the public services in an effort to wipe out institutional racism. The police, prisons, schools, hospitals, councils and other public bodies cannot adopt policies that even unintentionally have the effect of discriminating against one section of the community.

In groups

Discuss what you learn from these two stories about being the victim of a racial attack and racial harassment.

Racial attacks and the harassment

If someone abuses or threatens you or damages your property because of your colour, nationality or ethnic origin, that is **racial harassment**.

If someone uses any kind of physical violence against you because of your colour, nationality or ethnic origin that is **racial attack**.

Any of the following incidents are classified as a racial attack or harassment:

- personal attacks of any kind
- written or verbal threats or insults
- damage to property
- graffiti.

Victims of racism

'Don't they have any feelings?'

"Things are bad for my whole family at the moment. There's not one of us who hasn't had a problem, mum and dad included. We're not the only Bengali family in our area, but we seem to get most of the abuse from neighbours. They have no respect and put rubbish through our letterbox and smash bottles outside the front door. When my sister got married we went to the cars and a gang of lads who hang around the flats started to shout abuse – on her wedding day. Don't they have any feelings? We have reported things but we don't have any proof of who is harassing us. I'm determined these people will be punished one day with the help of the authorities."

Jonas, 15, East London

'I thought they were my friends'

"When Jason and I started going out, a few of my 'friends' made comments about me being better off with a white bloke. Then I started to get abusive phone calls, so I got the police involved. They traced the calls to a girl I thought was a good friend. We'd been to a school where there were people of all colours. I never thought of her as a racist."

Melissa, 17, West London

If you think racism is wrong, you can do something about it.

Many of us can probably remember times when we witnessed racist behaviour and did nothing to stop it. Maybe it was an incident at school, or a comment overheard at a party, or jokes and insults directed at other passengers on a bus or a train. It might even have come from a friend or relative, or a colleague, someone we respected. So we let it go. We didn't want to make a fuss. What difference would it make anyway?

The answer is: it can make all the difference.

By not speaking up you let others believe that their behaviour is acceptable. By speaking out, you can make them think about their words and actions. You may even stop them doing again.

Sometimes all it takes is a few quiet words to make someone realise they are out of order.

If you see someone being harassed, or overhear someone making racist remarks – maybe in the canteen or in

TAKE A STAND AGAINST RACISM

the playground at school, or at a sports or leisure centre – tell someone such as a manager or teacher. They are responsible for doing something about it.

If someone is being racially abused or attacked in the street or another public place, you should report the incident directly to the police, without delay.

Be careful that you do not do anything that will put yourself or anyone else in danger. If you think a situation could get out of hand, get help as quickly as possible.

If you hear racist chanting at a football match, or another sports event, report it to the club or the appropriate sports authority.

If you see racist graffiti on a building, train or bus, complain to the owners and ask for it to be removed.

If you think a TV or radio programme, an advertisement or a newspaper article is insulting to people from a certain ethnic group, write to the editor, producer or company involved.

It's up to all of us to make sure racist behaviour and attitudes are not accepted in Britain.

What should I do?

"My older brother has started to go round with a racist gang. He's picking up their attitudes. How can I stop him from becoming a racist bully?" George

"I've just started a new job. The other people there keeping making racist remarks about one of the girls because she's Asian. I'd like to do something about it, but I'm scared I'll antagonise them or that I'll even lose my job. What should I do?" Sasha

"It's easy to know what you ought to do if you see a racist incident, but in practice it can be hard to do the right thing." Mike

"Reporting a racist incident in the playground is not telling tales, it's the responsible thing to do and the only way to stamp out racism." Jamila

In groups

1 Discuss what advice you would give to George and Sasha.

2 Discuss Mike and Jamila's views. Share any experiences you have had of witnessing racist incidents and say what action you took.

Role play

In pairs, role play a scene involving two friends, one of whom quietly but firmly points out to the other that they are out of order because they've made a racist comment.

For your file

Write an email to a newspaper saying why racism is unacceptable and why we must all make a stand against it.

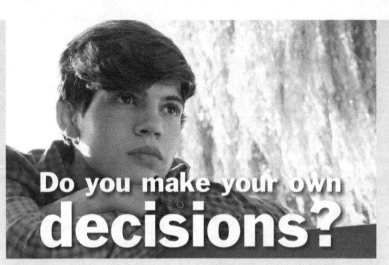

Do you make your own decisions?

How good are you at making up your own mind? Do you make your own decisions, or do you rely on other people, such as your parents, to help you? Do you wait to see what your friends are going to do before you commit yourself?

Answer this quiz to see how good you are at making your own decisions. Keep a record of your answers. Then check your score and discuss with a friend what you have learned about yourself from your answers.

1 Some kids in your street play jokes on an elderly person.
What do you do?

a Try to convince them it's an awful thing to do.
b Ignore it, it's none of your business.
c Go along with them because they say it's OK.

2 Your parent says that your best friend is a bad influence.
What do you do?

a Decide if he's a good friend, then give your parent a chance to get to know him better.
b Hang out with him behind your parent's back.
c Drop your friend because your parent says to.

3 You're not feeling very well, but your mates want you to go swimming.
What do you do?

a Decide whether you're well enough, then give them your answer.
b Ask a parent to come up with an excuse.
c Go with them because they want you to.

4 The council want to build on the only green playing space near where you live.
What do you do?

a Decide if it's worth saving your play area, ask for more information and see what others in the neighbourhood think.
b Wait for someone else to do something about it.
c Nothing, because you don't care.

5 Some friends are poking fun at the way someone speaks and making jokes about their accent.
What do you do?

a Challenge your friends and try to persuade them to stop.
b Shrug it off, because it's not your problem.
c Join in because you don't want to lose their friendship.

What's your score?

All or mostly as:
You can make decisions for yourself and then act on them.

All or mostly bs:
You like sitting on the fence rather than making a decision. While it's good that you listen to others, you should assert yourself more.

All or mostly Cs:
You need to exercise your mind; you're not using it at all. Others are doing your thinking for you.

In groups

What are the most important things to remember when you're making a decision?

● Honesty
● What your friends will think
● Respect for yourself and other
● Staying safe
● Tolerance
● Looking tough
● Fairness
● That you're right and everyone else is wrong

Add to this list any other things you think are important, and ran them in order of importance. Then share your views in a class discussion.

how to make decisions

Who influences you?

Study the diagram (right). It shows the people who may play a part in your life. Which of them influences you the most? On a piece of paper write down *five* people who influence you. Put them in order, starting with the person who influences you the most.

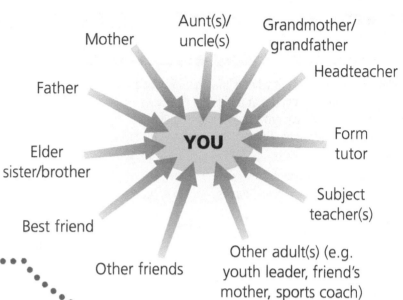

Mother
Aunt(s)/ uncle(s)
Grandmother/ grandfather
Headteacher
Father
YOU
Form tutor
Elder sister/brother
Subject teacher(s)
Best friend
Other adult(s) (e.g. youth leader, friend's mother, sports coach)
Other friends

Why do they influence you?

That person influences me because they ...

know how I feel

are willing to support me   understand me

are experienced

have time for me   will listen to me

are older than me

are concerned about me

always tell me the truth

have the same interests as me   are responsible for me

give me no choice

are someone I respect

know what I want   expect me to fit in with their ideas

In groups

1 Individually, go through the list of reasons (above). Beside the names of the five people who influence you, write down the reasons why. (They may be different from the reasons given in the box above.) Then, form groups and discuss who influences you and why.

2 List some of the important decisions a 14-year-old has to make. Talk about them one-by-one. Discuss whose advice you would listen to when making each decision.

For your file

Write about a time when you had a difficult decision to make and you asked people for their advice. Say whose opinion influenced you the most and why. Looking back, do you think you made the right decision?

Consider the consequences

When we try to work out what is the right or wrong thing to do, we often find that things aren't always straightforward. As we grow up we begin to discover what is right and wrong. Some of the ways we discover these things are:

by consequence:
If I do such and such a thing, this is likely to happen.

by example:
Watching how other people behave and copying them.

by experience:
If you do something, you find out what happens. This will affect what you do in the future.

by following rules:
Many rules have been made to try to protect people.

by our feelings:
If somebody hurts me I may (or may not) hurt somebody else because I know what it feels like.

When we make decisions about what to do we have to ask ourselves the following questions:

1 How will my decision affect me?

2 How will my decision affect my family and friends?

3 How will my decision affect my community?

4 How will my decision affect the world?

Long-term consequences: Tracey's story

Sometimes when somebody does something, the consequences of that action can stay with that person for the rest of their life. It is very important that we think about long-term consequences, because a wrong action or decision can ruin lives.

When Tracey was 16-years-old she got very drunk at a party. She had unsafe sex with an older man she didn't know. A few months later she began feeling ill and was diagnosed HIV positive.

Right and wrong

"There are certain things that are morally right or wrong, no matter who you are or what your beliefs are."

"Your ideas of right and wrong depend on what your religion is and what your beliefs and values are."

"What's right or wrong depends on the circumstances. For example, it's wrong to steal, but if you're starving you may have no choice."

"It can never be right to do something that hurts or harms someone else."

"What's right or wrong is up to the individual. You may have to break the law rather than do what your conscience tells you is wrong."

In groups

Discuss these ideas of right and wrong. Give reasons to support your views.

For your file

Write a statement for your folder in which you list examples of behaviour you think is wrong, explaining why.

Stay in control of your life

Don't let friends push you into doing something with them that you'd never dream of doing on your own. You owe it to yourself to make your own decisions rather than to allow others to make your decisions for you. It can be hard to say 'no', but not only will you respect yourself for doing so, other people will respect you too.

What Is peer pressure?

Peer pressure is when friends or people your age try to encourage you to do something because they're doing it. Quite often it is something that is illegal or at least likely to cause strife. It's important to understand why your friends are so eager for you to join them; it's not because they want you to be the same, but because they don't want you to be different.

These are the areas in which peer pressure is exerted, for example, having sexual relationships, drinking alcohol, smoking, drug taking, shoplifting, skiving off school, lying, and driving without a licence.

Your friends might try to tempt you into these things by saying that you're a wuss if you don't. They may also give you the cold shoulder and threaten to spread nasty gossip unless you do what they want you to do. They may try very hard to make sure that you are in a position where you can't say no.

If you have a friend or a group of friends who are trying to force you to break the law, take drugs or do anything else that you don't really want to do, you need to ask yourself this: are these people really your friends?

What to do when making decisions

Use this five-point plan whenever you are faced with making an important decision.

F Find out all the facts you need to know. The more information you have, the easier it is to come to a wise decision.

A Consider what the alternatives are. What are the different courses of action open to you?

C Consider the consequences of each course of action. Ask other people what they think and listen to the reasons they give for their views.

T Make up your own mind and take action. Take the decision which you think is right.

S Having made the decision, study the effects of your decision. If things don't turn out as you expected, then be prepared to reconsider your decision after a while. But don't act too hastily and don't change your decision just because you encounter a difficulty.

You can use the letters in the word **FACTS** to help you to remember what to do when making decisions.

Role play

Discuss situations in which someone may have to make a tough decision because their friends are pressurising them to do something they do not want to do. Talk about different ways of dealing with the situation and role play a scene in which a young person stays in control and resists the pressure to do something they do not want to do.

19

Parents and teenagers

There are tensions and conflicts at times in all families. It's a part of family life. Part of becoming an adult is learning to understand what causes arguments between parents and teenagers and how to deal with them.

Top ten causes of tension between parents and teenagers

1 The state of your bedroom.
2 The clothes you want to have and wear.
3 The volume of the music you listen to.
4 The people you choose as your friends.
5 Your failure to do your share of household chores.
6 The time you come in at night.
7 The amount of time you spend watching TV.
8 The words you use and the way you speak.
9 The amount of time you spend on the phone.
10 How much homework you do.

In pairs

1 Discuss the things that cause conflicts between parents and teenagers. In your experience, what are the top three issues that cause tension between them?

2 Do you think parents try to control teenagers' lives too much? How much independence do you think parents should give teenagers?

How to deal with differences

One way that you can try to avoid conflict between parents and teenagers is to draw up and agree a list of ground rules. Here's the start of a list of ground rules that Dave (14) and his parents drew up:

> Dave's room
>
> We agree that your room's your own and that we won't come in without knocking or asking your permission.
>
> You agree that you will take responsibility for it, changing the sheets regularly and doing a big clean-up at least once a month.
>
> You agree that you'll not leave your things lying around the rest of the house and will help to keep it tidy.

Draft details of other ground rules that Dave might have drawn up, for example about homework, going out with his friends, using the phone, playing his music.

How to get on better

Here's what some people had to say when asked to suggest things that parents and teenagers could do in order to get on better.

> "Most parents are very supportive. The trouble is that they are so concerned that they are often over-protective. If only they'd let teenagers be more independent, they'd have fewer arguments and everyone would be less stressed."

> "I think that communication between parents and teenagers is the crucial thing. If they spent more time together, for example by sitting down and having meals together and talking rather than watching TV, there'd be more understanding and less arguments."

In groups

Discuss these viewpoints. Suggest other things that you think parents and teenagers could do to help them get on better.

Educate **your parents**
by Philip Hodson

One thing I say is that children sometimes need to educate their parents. Educating your parents means showing them, by behaving in an adult way, that you are ready for a bit more freedom than they realised. They are only going to treat you in a grown-up way if you:

● learn to negotiate

● don't make angry demands

● give them reasons for your viewpoint

● show that you have researched the problem.

So when your dad is nagging at you because you want to go to a gig till midnight, show him that you have thought about how to get there safely, how to get back, how to pay for it and why you deserve this treat.

In pairs

Discuss the advice which Philip Hodson (above) and Erica Stewart (right) give on how to behave in an adult way. What do you think are the most useful pieces of advice?

Role play

Choose a situation in which a parent and teenager are clashing over what the parent sees as a piece of unacceptable behaviour by the teenager. Role play the scene twice – first showing the teenager reacting in a childish way, then showing the teenager behaving in a more adult way.

For your file

Write two versions of a story describing an argument between a teenager and one of their parents. (You could base it on a real-life incident.) In one version show the argument ending in a full-scale row. In the other version show it being resolved.

Arguments
and how to survive them

Erica Stewart offers advice on what to do when you and your parents have a difference of opinion.

1. Keep calm. Shouting at them isn't going to get your views across. It's only likely to make the argument develop into a full-on row.

2. Consider what's causing the disagreement. Is it a big deal that's worth having a major argument about? If it's not, then why not back down?

3. Say exactly how you feel and why you feel that way. Don't just make general accusations like, 'You never let me do what I want!'

4. Stick to the point. Don't bring up past disputes. Concentrate on the issue at hand.

5. Listen to their point of view. Try to understand where they are coming from and if they are just nagging because they are concerned for your welfare.

6. Be prepared to compromise. This shows that you are adult enough to understand that arguments occur because people have different viewpoints and that the way to resolve them is to find some middle ground.

7. Remember that you may not be in the right. For example, maybe your music was a bit loud and they've got a case for feeling annoyed.

8. Be prepared to say sorry. If you did lose it, storming off in a rage, then an apology is in order. It's hard to do, but it's the adult thing to do.

Rights and responsibilities

As you become an adult, you become aware of your **rights**. But it is important to realise that having rights also means having **responsibilities**.

My bill of rights

Everyone has rights, and though priorities may be different there are many 'expectations' that we hold in common. Some of these are included in the following list:

- I have a right to be treated well
- I have a right to be listened to
- I have a right to ask for something, even though I might not get it
- I have a right to privacy
- I have a right to make up my own mind
- I have a right to be happy
- I have a right to be different.

In pairs

1 On your own, copy out the bill of rights and add any others that are important to you. List them in order of importance, then compare your list with your partner's.

2 Talk about how you feel when one of your rights is denied you. Discuss how important it is to respect other people's rights.

For your file

Make a copy of your bill of rights. Write this statement underneath your list: 'In return for these rights, I will respect the rights of others.'

In groups

"The best way to deal with a problem involving your brother or sister is to get your parents to help you deal with it."

"It's better to deal with it yourself, but don't threaten them or try to bribe them. The way to get them to change their behaviour is to talk through the problem."

Discuss these views. What do you think is the best way to deal with a problem caused by your brother or sister? Should you try to deal with it yourself or is it better to get your parents involved too?

Coping with brothers and sisters:
Top ten causes of tension between brothers and sisters

1. Borrowing your things without asking permission
2. Failing to respect your privacy
3. Arguing over the use of either the computer or the TV
4. Disturbing you when you're busy
5. Saying embarrassing things or putting you down
6. Wanting you to play with them/help with their homework
7. Arguing about whose turn it is to do the chores
8. Getting in the way when you have friends around
9. Manipulating you by threatening to tell your parents something
10. Saying/doing things that they know irritate you and wind you up.

Taking responsibility

Part of becoming an adult is learning to take responsibility within the family. Exactly what this involves will depend on your family circumstances, says Fiona Johnson.

FOR ELLA it meant looking after her two younger brothers, while her mum was recovering from a serious illness.

"I was only 12 at the time, but there was no one else who could do it. Our dad left years ago and we've no close relatives. My mum's friend came in when she could, but she's got a full-time job and because she's a manager she has to work long hours. Having to cope made me realise just how much mum did for us all. Now she's better I still help her much more than I ever did before she was ill."

FOR RAJ it means taking responsibility for walking the dog twice a day.

"My dad used to do it, but then he got a promotion, which means that he has to be out of the house by 7 o'clock and he's often not back till late. So we had this family conference and it was quite clear that no one else could do it, so I said I'd be responsible for taking him out. Actually I quite enjoy it now – except when the weather's awful – but it's good exercise."

FOR JASON it means calling in to see his grandad twice a week, just to check he's OK.

"Since gran died, grandad's been living on his own and finding it very difficult to cope. So mum used to call in and see him every day on her way home from work. We could all see it was getting her down. So I said I'd call in twice a week as those are the days I go to football practice and he lives near the park where we go. As a result I've got to know grandad and mum says it does him a power of good to see me. Sometimes I go round at weekends now to save her visiting then too."

You can sometimes ease the pressures on other family members by taking responsibility and behaving in an adult way.

All these young people acted in an adult way because, in their different ways, they realised that they could do something that would help support the other people in their families. Being a teenager can be difficult. There are all sorts of pressures on you. But other members of your family have pressures on them.

Who's responsible?
by Derek Stuart

How much do you really do for yourself? Could you take more responsibility for the little things in life?

- Who buys your toothpaste?
- Who checks that your bike is safe to ride?
- Who washes your games kit?
- Who makes your packed lunch?

Teenagers often complain that their parents won't let them live their own lives. Then they complain when things aren't done for them.

If you answered 'I do' to all four questions at the beginning of the article, then maybe you really have begun to take responsibility for your own life. If not, then either stop whinging or do something about it.

In groups

1 What do 'being responsible' and 'taking responsibility' mean?

2 Discuss what you learn from Fiona Johnson's article about young people taking responsibility within their families. Share experiences of times when you have taken responsibility for something within your families.

3 Talk about what Derek Stuart says in his article. Say why you agree or disagree with his view. Who do you think should be responsible for the 'little things in life' – you or someone else in your family?

Your human rights

Civil liberties are the agreed list of human rights which the government must follow in order to treat you fairly. Your civil liberties protect you by limiting the powers of the government to force you to do things against your will. They enable you to say what you think and to practise whatever religion you choose.

Examples of civil liberties include:

Freedom from arbitrary arrest

Freedom from arbitrary detention

The right to a fair trial

Freedom of association

Freedom to protest

Freedom of movement

Freedom of conscience

Freedom of religion

Freedom of speech

Freedom to take part in elections

Freedom to live in safety

The right to privacy

Civil liberties are respected in democratic countries, such as in the UK, but are denied to people who live in undemocratic countries, such as North Korea, which are governed by a dictator.

French citizens like the lady pictured above have a passport and an identity card.

Protecting your civil liberties

Should everyone in the UK have to have an identity card?

In many countries everyone has to have an identity card. In some countries, it is compulsory to carry it at all times. The government made plans to introduce an identity card for everyone in Great Britain, but the plans were dropped because it was seen as an infringement of people's liberties.

The pressure group Liberty, which campaigns to protect civil liberties, argued that it would be ineffective in reducing crime, unfair, costly to introduce (around £5 bn) and intrusive by storing information on a government database that was personal and private.

In groups

What would your life be like if you were to be denied your civil liberties, as happens in a dictatorship? For example, how would your education be different? How would your family life be different? Which of the freedoms listed above would you miss the most?

In groups

"Identity cards would only contain what's on a person's passport anyway. What's all the fuss about? Everyone over the age of 14 should be issued with an identity card."

Discuss whether you agree or disagree with this view and say why.

CCTV
A cause for concern?

There are estimated to be over 2 million CCTV cameras in Britain, making it one of the most watched-over countries in the world. CCTV cameras at airports, railway stations and government buildings play an important role in counter-terrorism strategy.

CCTV is also used to reduce crime in public areas and there are 100,000 CCTV cameras in schools.

Most CCTV cameras are installed without public consultation and there is nothing to prevent your neighbour from fitting a CCTV system on his property for security purposes.

CCTV to be installed in Oxford Taxis

All conversations in Oxford taxis are to be recorded by CCTV in order to protect taxi drivers. The recordings will only be accessed if a crime is committed.

'It's an absolute invasion of privacy,' said Nick Pickles of the campaign group Big Brother Watch.

'The risk of intrusion is acceptable compared to the public safety benefit,' said Louisa Dean, a council spokesperson.

Oxford Mail

Mosquito alarms

The mosquito alarm is a device which emits a high frequency tone that is harmless but very irritating to those who hear it. The tone can only be heard by people aged under 25. It has been designed to be used in places where young people cause a nuisance by loitering in groups, for example in subways, shopping precincts or outside people's homes. It has been used by some local police forces, shop-owners and homeowners, who have found it has helped to cut down anti-social behaviour.

Campaigners argue it should be banned as it discriminates against young people and is an infringement of their rights. Also, it is heard by young people who are not loitering, but simply passing by.

Thousands of the alarms have been sold in the UK. But some local councils, such as Edinburgh, have banned their use.

In groups

"CCTV has made public places safer. The benefits outweigh the disadvantages."

"There needs to be more control of where CCTV is used."

Discuss these views.

In groups

Are mosquito alarms a good way of curbing anti-social behaviour or should they be banned?

Give reasons for your views.

For your file

Research the organisation Liberty and write a short statement about its aims and the campaigns it is currently running.

Protecting your rights

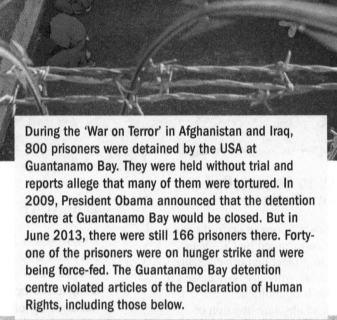

One of the most important roles any government has is to protect its citizens. Since terrorists act without any regard for the most basic human right – the right to life – governments sometimes take actions that restrict the freedoms of the few in order to protect the many.

It is a human right not to be imprisoned unless you are charged with a serious offence and given a fair trial. But in order to combat terrorism, the government allows terrorist suspects to be detained without charge for up to 28 days.

However, most people believe that some rights are so fundamental, such as the right not to be tortured, that no government can ever be justified in depriving anyone of this right, even terrorists.

Can torture ever be justified?

Some people argue that in certain circumstances torture can be defended as a 'necessary evil'. In the case of terrorists or enemy agents, they say, torture can be justified because it is a way of getting information quickly and, perhaps, saving more people from suffering as a result. Others argue that torture is inhumane and morally wrong and that the pain and suffering of the victim cannot be justified.

During the 'War on Terror' in Afghanistan and Iraq, 800 prisoners were detained by the USA at Guantanamo Bay. They were held without trial and reports allege that many of them were tortured. In 2009, President Obama announced that the detention centre at Guantanamo Bay would be closed. But in June 2013, there were still 166 prisoners there. Forty-one of the prisoners were on hunger strike and were being force-fed. The Guantanamo Bay detention centre violated articles of the Declaration of Human Rights, including those below.

The Universal Declaration of Human Rights was drawn up by the United Nations in 1948. It consists of 30 articles. Below is a summary of 3 key articles:

Article 5 No one shall be subjected to torture or to cruel, inhuman or degrading treatment or punishment.

Article 9 No one shall be subjected to arbitrary arrest, detention or exile.

Article 10 Anyone accused of breaking the law is entitled to a fair and public hearing.

The Universal Declaration of Human Rights

In groups

What do you think about the morality of torture? Organise a debate on the motion 'This house believes that there are no circumstances in which the use of torture can be justified.'

For your file

Find out about Amnesty International and its campaigns to seek the release of prisoners of conscience and people imprisoned without trial. Write a short statement about its work for your file.

Freedom of expression

In Britain, citizens are generally able to express their opinions and to practise their religion without fear of persecution. We take it for granted that we can go on the internet, send an e-mail or chat to a friend or search the web for information on any topic we like.

However, there are many countries, such as China, Iran, North Korea and Syria where people are denied these freedoms. For example, in Iran millions of websites, including news and social networking sites, are blocked.

Recording your every move

In 2012 the Home Secretary Theresa May introduced a draft Communications Bill that would have allowed the police to monitor all internet use in the UK. She argued that it would help the security agencies to track down terrorists and paedophiles. 'You and your loved ones have the right to expect the government to protect you from harm,' she said.

Opponents said the bill was an infringement of people's civil liberties and labelled it a 'snoopers' charter'. It was eventually dropped from the government's programme.

> *'There is a fine but crucial line between allowing our law enforcement and security agencies access to the information they need to protect the country, and allowing our citizens to go about their daily business without a fear that the state is monitoring every move.'*
>
> Lord Blencathra

In groups

1 Discuss what freedom of expression means.

2 Does freedom of expression mean that you can say or publish what you want? What do you feel about people who put pornography or racist literature on the internet? Should they be allowed to do this or should they be banned? What types of material, if any, should be banned?

Jailed
for using the internet

'In countries around the world, governments are targeting bloggers, closing websites and censoring internet searches. The internet is the new front in the battle between those who would speak out and those who would stop them.'

Amnesty International UK Director Kate Allen.

In 2011, a Vietnamese blogger Ta Phong Tan, a Catholic ex-policewoman, was given a 10-year jail sentence for criticising the one-party Communist government in her blog.

In 2012, Bassel Khartabil, a software engineer, was arrested and imprisoned without trial for his opposition to internet censorship on Syria.

The Chinese government blocks websites that discuss Tibetan independence, Taiwanese independence, the 1989 Tiananmen Square protects, freedom of speech, certain religious movements, such as Falun Gong and many blogging websites. However, the spread of Chinese online social networks, such as Sina's Weibo which has 200 million users, offers new opportunities for people to challenge the denial of their right to freedom of speech.

For your file

How important is the right to freedom of expression? Write a short statement giving your views.

The rights of women

Women's rights in the UK

Sexual discrimination is unlawful under the Sex Discrimination Acts of 1975 and 1986. These Acts make it illegal to treat anyone less favourably, on the grounds of their sex, than a person of the opposite sex is treated in the same circumstances. Sex discrimination is not allowed in employment, education, the provision of goods, facilities and services, or in advertising.

Discrimination at work

The Sex Discrimination Acts have done much to ensure that women are less discriminated against by employers in terms of recruitment. Women have equal rights to enter most occupations. However, in a number of ways women are still losing out to men in the world of work.

A much higher percentage of women than men are in low-paid jobs. For example, over 90% of domestic staff and secretaries are women. Similarly, less than 10 per cent of surgeons and electrical engineers are women.

Although Article 23 of the Universal Declaration of Human Rights states that 'everyone has the right to equal pay for equal work', women's earnings still lag behind men's earnings for both manual and non-manual work.

While the number of female managers continues to increase, there are still far more male managers.

'Everyone is entitled to the same human rights.'

You should not suffer discrimination, or be deprived of your rights, because of your race, colour, sex, language, religion, sexual orientation or political opinions.'

Article 2 of the Universal Declaration of Human Rights

THE RIGHT TO FIGHT

In Britain, women in the armed forces are excluded from roles that involve direct combat situations, but can support frontline roles. In the USA and in five European states – Denmark, France, Germany, the Netherlands and Norway – they can now undertake combat roles.

In groups

1 Discuss the view that all positions in the armed forces should be open to women.

2 Why do you think there are still more men than women in high-paid jobs?

Women's rights around the world

The 20th century saw a huge advance in women's rights in many countries. But in the Middle East and parts of Africa and Asia, women still have few rights and are often denied an education and the right to make decisions about their own lives.

For your file

Imagine you live in a country which has not yet passed a law against domestic violence. Write a statement arguing that the government should pass a law immediately.

What is sexual harassment?

Sexual harassment involves sexual behaviour such as physical contacts and advances, sexually coloured remarks, sending lewd e-mails, showing pornography and sexual demands whether by word or action.

In groups

1 'Hitting your partner can never be justified, no matter what they have done.' Discuss this view.

2 'Some forms of sexual harassment are more serious than others.' 'All forms of sexual harassment are serious.' Discuss these views.

What do you think should happen to someone found guilty of sexual harassing a person a) at work b) in public?

Domestic

'Violence against women continues to persist as one of the most heinous, systematic and prevalent human rights abuses in the world.'
Ban Ki-moon, UN secretary general.

According to Amnesty International one in three women worldwide has been beaten, coerced into sex or abused in some other way.

In Pakistan, for example, some married women are at risk of being kicked, slapped, beaten or sexually abused if their husbands are not satisfied with their cooking or cleaning, or when the woman has 'failed' to bear a child, or has given birth to a girl instead of a boy.

But more and more women are beginning to stand up for their rights and are being given protection by laws.

At least **89** countries have passed laws against domestic violence.
104 countries have made marital rape a crime.
90 countries have provisions against sexual harassment.
97 countries prohibit trafficking in human beings.

violence

Bank accounts

Banks
what do they offer?

What's the best way to manage your money? More and more young people are deciding to put their money in a bank account. So what do banks offer young people and how do you choose which bank account to open?

Security
Your money is safer in a bank than it would be in a drawer in your bedroom. And you don't have to carry large amounts round with you all the time, so there's less risk of it getting stolen.

Access
There's easy access to your money if it's in a bank account. If you've got a cash card account, you can draw money out either from a bank branch or a cash machine.

Interest
Accounts for young people are usually savings accounts, so you'll be paid interest on your money while it's in the bank. The rate of interest you get varies from bank-to-bank, so it's worth shopping around before opening your account, to find out which bank offers the best rate of interest.

In pairs

Discuss what you learn from this page about bank accounts and say whether or not you think it's a good idea to have a bank account.

For your file

A friend is thinking of opening a bank account. Write to them explaining the advantages of having a bank account and what you have to do to open one.

So you want to open a bank account?
Your questions answered

Q How do I open an account?

A You'll need to complete an application form, then take it to the bank, together with some form of identification, such as your birth certificate or passport. You'll also need to confirm your address, which you can do by taking a gas, electricity or telephone bill addressed to your parent or guardian. And you'll need some money to pay into the account. There's often a minimum deposit, usually either £1 or £10.

Q How can I keep track of what's in my account?

A If it's a cash card account, you'll be sent a full statement on a regular basis, often every 3 months. You'll probably also be able to get mini-statements on request or from a cash card machine.

Q How often is interest paid?

A Interest is usually paid quarterly or twice a year. But remember that interest rates change, so it's worth checking them now and again so that you can work out how much interest you're going to get.

Q What happens if I lose my cash card? Can someone else use it?

A With a cash card you are given a PIN (personal identification number). Your pin protects you against fraud, if you lose your card. So don't tell anyone else your PIN number or even write it down anywhere – just memorise it.

If you lose your card, report it to the bank at once. Then they'll stop the card, and no one else will be able to draw money from your account.

Which bank is best for you?

Armed with £100 to deposit, Penny Wiseacre checked out what the banks had to offer in March 2013.

Barclays

Account name Barclays Plus

Penny says: An account with easy access to your money which can be opened with just £1.

Key Features:

- Cash card which can be used to make withdrawals of up to £50 a day at thousands of cash machines.
- Interest paid on whatever money you have in your account.
- Pocket money or your allowance can be paid straight into your account.
- Shopping can be made easy with a Barclays debit card.

Halifax

Account name: Expresscash

Penny says: Offers instant access to your money.

Key Features:

- Visa debit card.
- Access to your money at thousands of cash points.
- You can use your card to withdraw up to £300, to get mini statements and to top up your mobile.
- Reassurance that you can't go overdrawn.

HSBC

Account name: My Account

Penny says: My Account is a current account linked to a savings account called My Savings.

Key Features:

- Visa debit card available with your parents' permission, so that you can shop online and in shops and stores wherever you see the Visa sign.
- Spending limited to what is in your account.
- Monthly interest on your savings.
- Mobile phone top-ups at HSBC cash machines.
- 24/7 access to your account with Internet banking.
- Online tips on how to make the most of your money.

Lloyds

Account name: Under 19s Account

Penny says: An account which offers more to over 16s than under 16s.

Key Features:

- A cashpoint card giving instant access to your money 365 days a year.
- Interest paid on the money you have in your account.
- Weekly balance alerts to your mobile.
- You can use a post office to pay money into your account.
- A Lloyds Visa debit card.
- Internet and telephone banking when you're 16.

Santander

Account name: 11–15 Current Account

Penny says: Offers a good interest rate, but you must pay in some money each month.

Key Features:

- Visa debit or cash card with access to your money from Santander or LINK cash machines.
- Online banking for 24 hour access to your account.
- Interest paid on balances up to £500 but you must make monthly payments into your account.
- Free text and email alert service providing you with notice that your balance is low or that payments are due.
- No overdraft – so you needn't worry that you are spending money you don't have.

In groups

Discuss what each bank account offers. How similar are their services? List in order of importance what services you want a bank account from a bank account and decide which one you would choose and why.

Other ways of saving

If you're a serious saver, then there are many other ways of saving your money besides opening a bank savings account. These two pages describe a number of these ways of saving. Some of them offer higher interest rates than bank savings accounts, but often you will only benefit from them if you leave your money in them for a considerable length of time – several months or several years. While some of them may be appropriate for you now, others are designed for adults and may not be suitable for you until you are older.

Premium bonds

Premium bonds offer you the opportunity of winning tax-free prizes. There are two jackpot prizes of £1 million every month. The precise number of prizes each month varies according to the size of the prize fund. The prize fund for February 2014 was approximately £49 million and there were 1.8 million prizes. The chances of a £1 unit winning a prize were 26,000 to 1.

You can buy premium bonds at any post office. The minimum for each purchase is £100. Purchases over £100 must be in multiples of £10. Anyone can own premium bonds but you have to be 16 before you can buy them for yourself. If you're under 16 they can only be bought for you by your parents, grandparents or guardians.

If you put your money into premium bonds, you can take it out whenever you want. But the drawback about premium bonds compared to other ways of saving is that your money doesn't earn any interest, other than the prizes.

Fixed interest savings

National Savings and Investments (NS&I) offer a range of savings and investments, including Children's Bonds, which have a guaranteed fixed interest of 2.5% for five years. You must invest at least a minimum of £25. Because NS&I is backed by HM Treasury your savings are 100% secure, but you will lose interest if you want to take your money out before the five year period ends.

It is worth shopping around if you want to invest in a fixed interest bond. For example, the Halifax Kid's Regular Saver bond had a fixed interest rate of 6% over one year in June 2014. The minimum investment was £10.

 **In pairs**

A relative offers to buy you £10 worth of fixed interest savings certificates or £100 worth of premium bonds, on condition that you do not take the money out until you are 18. Discuss which form of savings you would choose and why.

Stocks and Shares

ISAs – individual savings accounts

ISAs are offered by many financial institutions, such as banks and building societies. They offer a form of tax-free savings for adults who would otherwise pay tax on the interest they earn from their investments. There are restrictions on the amount of money each individual can save in ISAs each year. From July 2014 the maximum amount you could put into ISAs each year was £15,000.

You can invest in the stock market by buying shares. When you buy shares in a company you own part of that company. The price you will have to pay for each share will depend on which company you are investing in. You can find the price of a company's shares in the finance section of a daily newspaper.

If a company does well, you will get paid a share of the profits each year. This payment is known as a dividend. The size of your dividend will depend on how many shares you own. Also, if the company is doing well, the value of your shares may go up. If so, you would be able to sell them for more than you bought them for.

However, if the company does badly, then the value of your shares will go down. If you sold them you would get less than you paid for them. If the company was to go bankrupt, you could lose all the money which you paid for the shares.

In groups

Discuss the advantages and disadvantages of the different ways of saving that are described on these pages. Choose two ways of saving that you would recommend – one for young people, one for adults.

For your file

Work with a partner. Go through the articles in this unit and pick out all the financial terms that are used, such as balance, dividend and premium. Write out definitions of them, if necessary using a dictionary to help you. Then put your glossary of financial terms in your file.

Coping with grief

How you may feel
after a death

Shock

You will nearly always feel shock after a member of your family or a close friend has died. Even though the person may have died after a long and serious illness it can still be a shock – all the more so if they died suddenly, in an accident, for instance. Part of being in shock is disbelief – you may not believe what has happened. You may find that you are somehow denying that it is really happening at all. You will probably feel numb at times. Many people react this way immediately after a death. Being in shock and 'denial' is a natural way of protecting us from being overwhelmed by too many painful feelings.

Sadness

Once the reality of the death has seeped in, you will probably feel a terrible sense of sadness, loss and loneliness. You may be very unhappy indeed, especially in the early days, and you may want to cry a lot. This sadness is one of the strongest feelings that you may have after someone dies. It is an important part of grieving, and not something to be bottled up (see page 20). However, the extremes of sadness should lessen gradually as time goes on.

Anger

You might feel angry as well – above all, angry with the person who has died for leaving you. This is perfectly natural, but anger is one of the most difficult feelings to admit to, even to yourself. That is why your anger may be directed towards others, for example doctors and nurses,

care-workers, other adults for not telling you in time that the person was dying – even at life itself for being so unfair. Anger only becomes harmful if you begin to feel it all the time, or if you always turn it against yourself in a punishing way. You will get less angry as time passes.

Resentment

Resentment is a kind of slow-burning anger that can build up over a long period. Young people often feel resentful if one of their parents dies: there may new responsibilities that you don't want to – or feel unable to – take on. You may resent your friends their easier life with two parents. Remember, though, that you need your family and friends around you, so try not to let resentment come between you and spoil your relationships.

Guilt

People very often feel guilty after the death of someone important to them. You may catch yourself thinking 'If only ...' if only you had been kinder to them in the last few months; if only you had been able to tell them that you really loved them. This regret is a way of reviewing the past and trying to make sense of it. You may feel more guilt and self-blame if you have argued a lot with the person before their death. Try not to feel guilty about this, because such arguments are a normal part of your growth into an independent adult.

Worries and fears

The death of someone close to you can

also make you fearful about the future. The world may seem a very unsafe place to be in: who will be the next person to fall ill, or have an accident, or die? Maybe even you? These worries and fears are again quite normal, and they do get less strong over time.

Time

Time is such an important factor with so many of the feelings described in this section. You need time to express the feelings, time to work them through, and a lot of time before they stop dominating your life.

 **In groups**

Discuss what you learned from this article about the different feelings people who are bereaved have and why they have them.

Funerals

Different cultures and religions have different mourning customs. Whatever form the funeral service takes, it is important because a funeral is the public recognition of the end of the person's life. Everyone who has loved or known the person gathers together to show how they cared for him or her and to share their grief. Some people express their grief by crying, others don't. A funeral is a sad occasion, but it is also an occasion to remember and celebrate the person's life.

> **"When my gran died, the funeral was really moving. It was sad, of course, but her best friend gave a speech about what a fun person she'd always been and they played her favourite music."**
> **– Soosan**

Showing *emotions*

How should you express your feelings of grief when someone close to you has died? Should you let it all out – and for how long? Should you keep it under wraps and hope it will go away?

We all have different ways of showing our feelings. Not everyone wants to cry a lot; some people are very quiet and hide their feelings; other people like to talk about the person who has died. Often we are told what feelings to have, or how to show them, but this can be very different from what we actually feel.

We may be told by our parents or relatives to be 'brave' or 'strong'. There is a long tradition in many western countries for people to suffer grief in private, not to burden others with it or to be too emotional in public. But this isn't necessarily the best way to deal with difficult feelings, nor is it the only way. The tradition in many other parts of the world is for people to cry in public, to be openly emotional and to share their feelings with others.

It is certainly not a sign of weakness if you feel like crying. Indeed, it can be a sign of deep feeling. It is also a great relief and it can help other people to show their sympathy for you. So you should definitely cry if that is what you feel like doing. The expression of grief through your tears may bring you a lot of relief.

However, there are other ways of grieving than crying. Thinking about the person you have lost is also a way of grieving. And so is thinking about how the world is now that they aren't there for you. Talking about these thoughts and feelings may be difficult, but it is good to try, as it will move the process on and give you some relief.

There are other ways of showing our emotions that are less helpful, such as being destructive or very negative towards others. But talking about your grief instead is a more appropriate way of dealing with the difficult feelings inside. It is also much more helpful to you.

In pairs

ometimes young people are not expected to go to a neral or are prevented from doing so by adults. What e the arguments for and against letting children attend nerals? Who should make the final decision – e children themselves or their parents? Does it depend hose funeral it is or how old the child is?

In groups

Study the article 'Showing emotions'.

Why is it important to cry if you feel like crying?

Why is it a good idea to talk to someone about your feelings?

Helping the bereaved

It can be hard to know how to help someone who is grieving. Here's a test to help you understand how you can support someone who has been bereaved.

Can you help a friend in need?

1 When your friend brings up the subject of the person who has died, the best thing for you to do is …
a Listen.
b Try to change the subject.

2 When you see your friend for the first time after they've been bereaved, the best thing you can do is …
a Avoid the subject of bereavement at all costs.
b Say something about the death as soon as you meet.

3 Your friend and her family would probably appreciate …
a A quick call to ask if there's anything you can do to help.
b A bit of peace and quiet with no interference from people outside the family.

4 When should your friend have got over the grief?
a After six months.
b Probably never.

5 If you do write a card or letter, it's more comforting to …
a Include a little note sharing some memories.
b Simply sign your name rather than write a message.

6 If you're one of the first people to find out what happened, you should …
a Keep the news to yourself.
b Let other people know as soon as possible.

Answers below

Answers

1 (a) Listen. It's important to let them know you are there if they'd like to talk about their feelings, or about the person who has died, even if you didn't know them.

2 (b) Say something. Don't avoid bringing up the subject when you first meet for fear of 'reminding' your friend about their grief. Let them know you're aware of the situation and that you're ready to lend support.

3 (a) A quick call. Why not ask if their family would like you to help with practical things? It could be anything from offering to sort out shopping to keeping an eye on

4 (b) Probably never, although things will improve as time goes by. Don't lose patience with your friend if you feel it's taking too long for him or her to get over the grief. Take more time to listen and talk things over.

5 (a) Write a note, saying how sorry you are to hear the sad news. If you knew the person who died, you might like to share some memories you have of them.

6 (b) Let other people know. If you are one of the first to know, it's a good idea to let their other close friends know, so that they can offer their sympathy and support.

pets when they attend the funeral, but every little bit helps.

Someone to talk to

If you are upset about the death of someone close to you, you could contact Cruse Bereavement Care, a national charity that offers support to anyone who has suffered a bereavement.

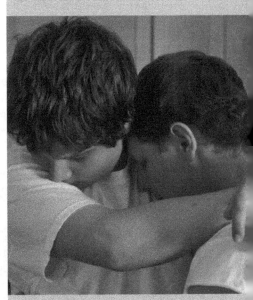

Contact Cruse Helpline
0844 477 9400

"People who contact us usually want to talk about the person who's died and we'll listen. They can say whatever they like about them. They'll often want to talk about other feelings surrounding the death – maybe they'll feel angry or wish they'd told them something while they had the chance."

"Everyone grieves in their own way, but when you feel ready, it can help to talk to someone – they can either be someone close or a stranger. Some people find it easier to talk to a stranger. Call us any time and we'll help you along the way." – Cruse

In groups

Discuss what you learn from the advice on this page about how to help someone who has been bereaved.

Coping with rejection

Erica Stewart offers advice on how to deal with rejection

When a relationship breaks up, it can be a very painful experience, especially if it happens suddenly when you weren't expecting it. The shock you feel can be similar to the way you would feel in bereavement.

Coping with rejection isn't easy, and if the relationship was a really good one, it's natural to feel grief that it's over. So don't feel that it's wrong to get some of the grief out of your system by having a good cry.

One thing people often do if they're rejected is to start asking themselves what went wrong. It is worth remembering that relationships end for all kinds of reasons and that it's rarely just one person's fault. Being rejected hurts and dents your confidence, but beware of looking for faults in yourself that simply aren't there.

Also, don't waste time trying to repair a relationship that's over. If you go round pleading with your ex-boyfriend/girlfriend to take you back, you're only prolonging the agony. Doing so is more likely to turn them off than win them back.

And try not to sit around brooding and letting yourself think that you'll never make another relationship. As you go through your teens, you're likely to have a number of relationships. When a relationship ends, it can be difficult to tell yourself there'll be others. But there will be!

Time is a great healer. It might feel like you will never get over being dumped, but you will. Keeping busy helps. Make sure you arrange to go out with your friends and have some fun times. You may not feel like it, but it's better than moping.

Announcing it's over

The golden rule when ending a relationship is to make sure that you leave the other person's confidence intact. So try to avoid being too personal. If you're ending the relationship because you feel the other person has been too possessive or jealous, then it's worth saying so, as that may help them in future relationships. But if you've decided to end it because you don't like the person they are these days, there's no need to say so. It's bad enough being rejected, without having to listen to a string of hurtful remarks.

Louisa Fairbanks

In pairs

Discuss what Louisa Fairbanks says about how to end a relationship. What's the best way to announce that you are ending a relationship – over the phone, through a friend, by writing a letter or face-to-face?

In groups

Discuss the advice that Erica Stewart gives on how to cope with feeling rejected. Which is the most useful piece of advice?

Draw up a list of Dos and Don'ts when dealing with rejection.

For your file

A friend has emailed you to tell you that the person they've been going out with for over a year has ended the relationship and they are desperately upset. Write a reply offering them advice on how to cope with their feelings.

How dangerous is drugtaking?

Drug use can never be 100% safe. It always involves risks, though sometimes the risk is greater than others. How dangerous it is depends on the drug itself, the person taking the drug and how and where the drug is taken.

The risk will also depend on:

- **How much is taken.**
- **How strong the dose is**, for example two ecstasy tablets that look the same may have very different doses in them.
- **How often it is taken.**
- **What else might be mixed in with the drug**, especially the weird stuff that is often mixed with illegal drugs.
- **How a drug is taken;** injecting is the most dangerous way to use drugs – the dose is taken all at once so there is a danger of overdose – and if injecting equipment is shared, there is the danger of passing on infections like hepatitis and HIV (the virus that leads to AIDS).

THE PERSON

If you drink when you feel miserable, you will often feel worse, and if you are anxious and depressed before taking LSD, you are more likely to have a bad experience. Also the following factors may influence the experience:

- **Physical health problems.** Drug use could be more dangerous for those with heart, blood pressure, epilepsy, diabetes or liver problems.

- **Weight.** Drugs act differently depending how heavy you are: the effects may be more in a lighter person.
- **Not being used to drugs.** Somebody new to drug use may be anxious, unsure of what to do or expect and be more likely to get into problems or have a bad experience.

THE DRUG

Different drugs carry different risks.

Drugs such as heroin, alcohol or tranquillisers can lead to **physical dependence or withdrawal symptoms.**

Drugs like amphetamine, ecstasy and cocaine are **uppers** – they speed the body up – and can be particularly dangerous for people who have heart or blood pressure problems.

Drugs like heroin, alcohol and solvents are **downers** – they slow the body down – and can be very dangerous if mixed because the body can stop altogether. This is an overdose and can be fatal.

Others are **hallucinogens** (LSD, magic mushrooms) and can lead to people freaking out and doing dangerous things. Anybody with a mental illness should steer well clear of these drugs and also cannabis.

THE ENVIRONMENT

- **Where people use** drugs can be risky. Some take drugs in dodgy places, like canal banks, near railway lines, in derelict buildings. Accidents are much more likely in these places, especially if people are out of their heads.
- **What people are doing while they are on drugs** can be risky. Driving a car or bike or operating machinery while on drugs can greatly increase the chances of accidents. Having sex while on drugs can make remembering safer sex – like using condoms – much more difficult.

SO WHAT DOES ALL THIS MEAN?

It means that it is impossible to make simple statements like 'if you take this drug then this will happen.'

We are all individuals – what might be safe for one person could be dangerous for the next – or even dangerous for the same person in a different situation.

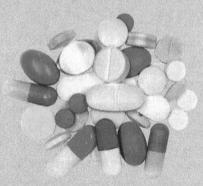

In groups

Discuss what you learn from this page about the different factors that affect how dangerous drugtaking is.

For your file

Write an article for a teen magazine based on the information on this page, explaining what makes drugtaking a risky business.

Should taking drugs be legalised?

Some people argue that certain drugs should be made legal and given the same legal status as alcohol and tobacco. Others argue for decriminalisation, which would mean that possession would not be a criminal offence, but might be subject to penalties like those for speeding or parking illegally.

Surveys suggest that most people would be in favour of seeing the personal use of cannabis decriminalised. But the majority of the public is firmly against altering the restrictions on heroin and cocaine.

Should cannabis be legalised?

Yes...

- It would take the supply of the drug out of the hands of violent criminals.
- For many users, cannabis is no more harmful than alcohol or tobacco, which are freely available.
- There might be an increase in users, but that also means a huge increase in tax revenue.

No...

- It could be a first step to more widespread, and potentially disastrous, legalisation of other drugs.
- It would lead to a large increase in use, which might put people on a 'slippery slope' to harder drugs.
- Some forms of cannabis are very harmful and have been implicated as a cause of mental health problems.

The benefits of legalisation

Many people may think that taking drugs is inherently wrong and so should be illegal. But there is a question of effectiveness – does making it illegal stop people doing it? The answer is no.

Drugs could be regulated in the same manner that alcohol and tobacco are regulated, and heavily taxed.

A sensible policy of regulation and control could reduce burglary, cut gun crime, reduce prostitution, clear out our overflowing prisons, and raise billions in tax revenue. Drug users could buy from places where they would be sure the drugs had not been cut with dangerous, cost-saving chemicals. There would be clear information about the dangers involved and on how to seek treatment.

In groups

Discuss the arguments for and against the legalisation of cannabis.

'Drugtaking is too dangerous to be legalised. People need to be protected from harming themselves by taking drugs.' Say why you agree or disagree with this view.

Do you think it should be up to individuals or the government to decide which substances they consume?

Drug problems

'My life's a mess'

Name: Sarah **Age:** 16 **Lives:** Suffolk

I used to think I'd never take drugs. I was happy enough – what did I need drugs for? If only things had stayed that way...

The first time I took speed I just wanted to try it once – to see what it was like. We were going to this party, and my friends said that we'd have a better night if we were off our heads. I can't remember much about the party now. I felt so tired afterwards – really done in.

Drug buddies

I started going out with these friends quite a bit – they knew where all the good parties were. We'd meet up on a Saturday night and take some MDMA to see us through. We had an amazing time. My other friends at school seemed really immature and boring.

Out of control

After school, we'd meet up and smoke some spliffs. I could never be bothered to do any homework when I got home – I always felt so tired. When I failed the end of year exams I had this massive row with my Dad. I hated being at school and I hated being at home. I started stealing money from my mum's purse to pay for the drugs and the nights out. I knew I was letting her down – but it had got so that I only felt good when I was off my head on something.

Disaster

There was this big night out planned but I was broke. Me and a mate went into town and nicked some stuff from one of the department stores to sell. I was really scared. We thought we'd got away with it, but then the store detective came up to me – it was the worst moment of my whole life.

Shunned

The police told my parents – and now my Dad won't speak to me. He says he never thought his daughter would turn out to be a thief. My friends at school have found out about the shoplifting and some of them are keeping away from me. I don't know how all this happened. I never thought I'd be in trouble with the police. It's going to take a long time before people trust me again – I just wish everything was back to normal.

How to help a friend who has a problem with drugs

We all need friends. Sometimes we need the help they can give us. Sometimes it's our turn to help them out. If someone you know has a problem with drugs ...

- Stick by them. Don't turn your back on them.
- Listen to them and how they say they feel.
- Don't start slagging them off to their face or other people.
- Suggest what they might do but don't keep on about it. They will have to make their own decisions.
- If they want, offer to go with them if they are going to seek help from a drug agency, doctor, counsellor or whoever.
- Encourage them to be positive about themselves.
- Encourage them to feel they can do something positive about their problems.

In groups

Discuss Sarah's story. Talk about how getting into drugs has affected her life. If you were Sarah's friend, what would you say to try to help?

For your file

Dear Melanie, My friend's got involved in the drug scene. She's got real problems. How can I help her? – Shania

Write the reply you would send to Shania if you were Melanie.

What to do in an emergency

Drug use can be dangerous and it's important that you know what to do in an emergency. The lives of friends and people around you could depend on you knowing basic first aid.

If people are tense and panicky

This tends to occur with hallucinogenic drugs like LSD and magic mushrooms, but it also happens with drugs like amphetamines and ecstasy as well as high doses of cannabis. If someone is really tense and panicky after taking drugs, take the following steps:

✔ Calm them down and reassure them.

✔ Talk quietly and explain that the panicky feeling will gradually go.

✔ Keep them away from loud noises and bright lights.

✔ Help them if they overbreathe (hyperventilate). When someone breathes very quickly and gasps for breath, they often get dizzy and feel sick.

If people overheat or dehydrate

This tends to happen with drugs like amphetamines and ecstasy when people really exert themselves. These drugs raise body temperature. Overheating and dehydration can result. This can be very dangerous and has been the main reason for ecstasy-related deaths.

The warning signs include: ● cramps in the legs, arms and back ● failure to sweat ● headaches and dizziness ● vomiting ● suddenly feeling very tired ● feeling like a pee but not doing much when you go ● fainting.

It can be prevented by:

✔ Avoiding amphetamines or ecstasy in the first place.

✔ Not dancing for long periods at a time; taking regular rests and relaxing in a cool area.

✔ Drinking water, fruit juice or a sports drink at about the rate of one pint an hour (sipping the drink regularly) and avoiding alcohol.

✔ Drinking or eating something that keeps the salt levels in the body up. Salty snacks, fruit juice, fizzy drinks and sports drinks will all help to keep the body provided with the minerals it needs.

✔ Wearing cool clothes and not wearing hats (hats keep heat in).

If someone is overheating:

✔ Move the person to a cool area – outside if possible.

✔ Splash them with cold water to cool them down.

✔ Call an ambulance. Explain to the ambulance crew what has happened and what you have done.

If people are drowsy but conscious

This usually happens with downer drugs like alcohol, tranquillisers and heroin, but can happen with solvents (glue and gas). If someone is really drowsy take the following steps:

✔ Put the person in the recovery position and keep talking to them.

✔ Try to stop them becoming unconscious and don't put them to bed as they might lose consciousness in their sleep.

✔ If they want a drink, only give them sips of lukewarm water.

✔ Call for medical assistance.

If people faint or lose consciousness

Give them emergency first aid, by putting them in the recovery position, checking their breathing and loosening any tight clothing that might restrict it, and call for an ambulance.

For your file

Draw a cartoon strip of an incident in which a teenager becomes ill after taking drugs. Show how the person is given first aid by their friends.

Young people and crime

Why do so many young people commit crimes?

One in three crimes of burglary, theft and criminal damage is committed by people under the age of 17. Most of these crimes are committed by boys. There are many reasons why some young people commit crimes. Here are some possible answers.

1 On television, in adverts, magazines and music, young people are encouraged to spend, spend, spend. They are told there is a certain way to look, a certain way to impress others. There is a lot of pressure on young people to behave in a certain way – these pressures lead some young people into crime.

2 Many people have very little money. Yet they live in a society that says money is important. If you've got no money and no prospects of a job or future, then crime might seem an attractive alternative.

3 Some people have very unhappy childhoods – violence at home, broken marriages, difficult parents. These can lead to some young people expressing their anger and frustration through crime.

4 For others, life seems boring and meaningless. They commit crimes because it brings adventure and risk into their lives and makes them feel they've got a purpose. They reach a stage where they don't care if they get caught – anything is better than a boring existence.

5 For some young people, a life of crime makes them feel important. They feel different from others – it makes them feel big. If a person belongs to a group or gang, they may feel that being involved in crime will gain them respect in the group.

Girls and crime

In 2007, the number of people aged 10 to 17 found guilty of, or cautioned for, criminal offences was 126 000. This number was down to 74 000 in 2010, the lowest since the data first became available in the mid 1990s.

Four times as many boys are cautioned or found guilty of offences as girls. However, the number of girls committing offences is higher than it has been historically. Theft accounts for two-thirds of crimes committed by girls and one-third of crimes committed by boys.

Jan Walsh, head of a Consumer Analysis Group, said: 'I believe the commercial society is a root cause. There is a much greater emphasis on what we possess today. From the earliest age, through television advertising and peer pressure, children are persuaded that they must possess all kinds of things. They must have the right trainers on their feet and the right logo on their backs. This didn't exist 50 years ago.'

Others argue that there is a difference in the way children are brought up. Girls 50 years ago had much less freedom. Consequently they were much less likely to get into trouble.

In groups

1 Discuss the reasons why young people commit crimes. Which of the five reasons given in the article above do you think is the main reason? Can you suggest any other reasons?

2 What does Jan Walsh mean by 'the commercial society' (see article, left)? Do you agree that young people are put under pressure to have possessions from an early age?

Shoplifting

A survey of youth crime showed that shoplifting came second to fare dodging as the most commonly committed crime.

Why do people do it?

There are many reasons why people shoplift. Greed is one, but some people do it because they find it exciting. Others do it to finance a certain lifestyle or drug habit, but shoplifting can also be an act of desperation by someone who needs clothes or food and has to steal out of necessity.

One of the most common reasons among teenagers is peer pressure. Perhaps your friends have encouraged you to do it for a laugh or because they do it and you think you should too. But remember, shoplifting, even if it's as small as a packet of chewing gum, is a criminal offence. And just because some of your mates manage to get away with it doesn't mean you will too. If you are spotted you'll have to live with the shame of being caught and having a criminal record. So when you're tempted, ask yourself, 'Is it really worth it?'

In groups

1 Discuss why Rebecca started to shoplift. What do you think are the main reasons why young people shoplift?

2 What is your attitude to shoplifting? Is stealing from a shop any different from stealing from an individual or from someone's home?

3 'Modern shops make shoplifting too easy.' What do you think shops and shopkeepers could do to cut down shoplifting?

4 What should shopkeepers do if they catch a shoplifter? Should they always call the police whatever the circumstances? Give reasons for your views.

Rebecca's story

"Getting caught was so humiliating"

I first started shoplifting properly when I was 12, although I'd stolen things like sweets before that. I started nicking because most of my mates used to do it in their lunch hour. We'd hang around the local shopping precinct and for a laugh see what we could steal.

Half the time we nicked things we didn't even want because it was a laugh just to see what we could get. I was so confident about robbing stuff that it never really crossed my mind that I might get caught. But one day last November I got a real shock.

One afternoon I bunked off school and went to steal some make-up. I used my usual technique to distract the assistant's attention and thought I'd got away with it. But as soon as I went through the exit a security guard grabbed me by the arm. He was really rough with me and I was practically dragged through the store with loads of people staring at me. I felt completely humiliated.

I was taken to an upstairs room to see the store manager. I thought he'd be okay if I made up some story and started crying, but he just didn't want to listen to me. I tried to tell him it was all a mistake but he told me I'd been filmed walking out of the store with goods I hadn't paid for and that another shopper had also witnessed me putting make-up up my shirt sleeve.

I was asked to turn out all my pockets and to undo my sleeves. I had three lipsticks on me that I hadn't paid for, and I had no receipts. When I tried to talk to the manager he just said, 'You can talk to the police when they get here.'

For your file

Write a story about a young person who is caught shoplifting.

Punishment

The aims of punishment

A person who is found guilty of a criminal offence will be given a punishment by the court. There are five main theories of punishment, each of which has a different purpose (see table).

In groups

Discuss the five theories of punishment. What do you think the most important aim of a punishment should be?

Imprisonment – does it work?

Taking away a person's liberty by giving them a custodial sentence is sometimes regarded as the best way not only to deal with people who have committed a serious offence or who are habitual offenders, but to teach a young offender a lesson. However, there is evidence from research studies to suggest that harsh punishments do not necessarily work. Instead of deterring a person from committing further crimes, a period of imprisonment may make them feel resentment towards society, so that on their release they commit further crimes in order to get their revenge. Whatever the reason, a large number of those who are given custodial sentences re-offend following their release.

Theory of punishment	Aim of punishment	Examples of punishment
1 Deterrence	To stop the offender from doing it again; to discourage others from committing a similar offence.	A prison sentence or a heavy fine.
2 Protection	To protect society by making it impossible for the offender to commit further offences.	Long prison sentences for dangerous offenders; banning dangerous drivers.
3 Reform	To help the offender change their behaviour, so that they will stop committing crimes.	Many sentences for young offenders, e.g. community service orders.
4 Retribution	To make the offender suffer for the crime.	Sentence proportionate to severity of the crime, e.g. at least five years for rape.
5 Reparation	To repay or compensate the victim.	Compensation orders and reparation orders.

In groups

"Prisons are necessary because they keep criminals out of circulation."

"You've got to have prisons because no other form of punishment acts as a sufficient deterrent."

"Community service is a better punishment than prison, because offenders are doing something to help the community."

"A prison sentence is more likely to turn a younger offender into a criminal than to reform him."

Discuss these views and say why you agree or disagree with them. What do you think should be the main reasons for giving someone a prison sentence?

Types of punishment

The punishment that can be given for any particular crime is determined by the law. So the punishment for the same crime can vary from country to country. For example, in Britain drug dealing is punishable by imprisonment and/or a fine, while in some countries it is punishable by death.

In groups

Study the cases below. Imagine that each person has been prosecuted and found guilty in court. What punishment would you regard as appropriate in each case **a)** if it is the person's first such offence, **b)** if the person already has a record suggesting that they are often in trouble?

1 A 20-year-old convicted of selling ecstasy and cocaine.

2 A 16-year-old who was found drunk and disorderly in a public place.

3 A 15-year-old who stole a car and crashed it, causing £5000 worth of damage.

4 An 18-year-old who mugged a middle-aged woman and stole her handbag.

5 A 15-year-old who was caught shoplifting a pair of designer trainers.

6 A 25-year-old convicted of rape.

7 A 17-year-old convicted of being in possession of a knife.

What about the victim?

Some people argue that the punishment should fit the crime and take into account the effect the crime has on the victim. In some cases, the effect of a crime on a victim may be out of all proportion to the crime itself. For example, the theft of £10 may completely destroy the confidence and security of an elderly person living alone. However, the theft of £20,000 worth of goods from a large wholesale company may make only a very small dent in the accounts.

A glossary of punishments

Here are some forms of punishment used around the world today

Attendance centres – part of the offender's leisure time must be spent here.

Binding over to keep the peace – the offender's parents must look after their child properly or face a fine.

Capital punishment – the death penalty.

Community service order – unpaid work for the community.

Compensation order – payment made by the offender to the victim.

Conditional discharge – no action is taken on condition that the offender does not reoffend within a set period.

Confiscation of property – goods or possessions are taken away.

Corporal punishment – beating or other physical punishment.

Custodial sentence – prison or other secure accommodation.

Disqualification – from driving, for example, or from holding office.

Fine – the amount depends on the offence, the age of the offender, their history and their ability to pay.

Probation order – the offender must be supervised by a probation officer and usually attend a day centre.

Reparation order – the offender must compensate the victim or the community in some way.

Supervision order – the offender must be supervised by a social worker or probation officer.

In groups

1 How do you decide which is the more serious crime? Should the burglar who stole £10 be punished more severely because of the effect on the victim? Or should the thieves who stole £20,000 get a heavier punishment because the value of the property stolen was so much greater?

2 Some of the victims of crime are relatively helpless (for example, a disabled older person, or a young child). Should the severity of the punishment take into account who the victim was, or should there be a standard punishment for a particular type of crime, irrespective of who the victim was?

Gang crime and knife crime

I'm being pressured into joining a gang, what can I do?

You don't have to do anything you don't want to do and no one has the right to force you into doing things that make you uncomfortable, or put you in danger.

You might feel that if you join a gang you'll be looked after and protected, but this is not always true. Sometimes being in a gang makes you a target for people and you might find yourself in danger, sometimes from other gangs.

If someone is trying to make you join a gang or become involved in their activities, you need to tell someone you trust, such as a parent or a teacher. It's important they know what is happening and they will be able to help you.

If you don't have anyone to tell or feel that you can't talk about it, you can call Childline on 0800 1111 and they can help.

Role play

In pairs, role play a scene in which a teenager confides in an older person that they are being pressurised to join a gang. The older person encourages them to resist the pressure. Before carrying out the role play, discuss as a class what the older person might say to the teenager.

Gang crime and knife crime

Young people may think that being in a gang will give them a glamorous lifestyle, but the reality is very different. Being in a gang puts you at more risk of committing crime, dealing or taking drugs, ending up in prison, being a victim of violence and even death.

Young people can join gangs for a number of reasons:
- to get recognition
- for excitement
- for friendship
- to be accepted
- to have a sense of belonging
- to get power over other people
- to get money from crime
- for protection
- to get respect
- to have their own territory.

In groups

Why do you think are the main reasons some people join street gangs? List the reasons given above in order of importance, adding any other reasons you can suggest.

Cutting down on knife crime

Here are some suggestions for solving the problems of knives and knife crime:

- metal detectors in schools
- paying students to report on others carrying knives
- bigger penalties for offenders
- more publicity about the dangers
- banning the sale of knives on the internet
- letting teachers search students bags and pockets.

Have your say about

Carrying knives

"A lot of young people who say that they are carrying knives don't really. They are just trying to scare those around them."

"Carrying a knife makes you feel safer."

"You are less likely to be bullied or attacked if you are carrying a knife."

"Knives are a problem – but the media makes the situation sound a lot worse than it is."

"If you want people to respect you, you have to carry a knife."

"Most people carry a knife for show. They don't intend to use it."

If you find yourself involved in a gang and your friends already carry knives or guns, you might feel under pressure to do so as well.

Your friends might tell you that you will be respected or feared for carrying a weapon. Maybe they say you need it for your protection. But all it really does is put you and your friends in greater danger.

What can you do?

The advice is clear – don't give in to them, **don't carry a weapon**.

If you don't take it with you, it can't be used.

While walking away is the hardest thing to do, it is the safest and won't get you in trouble with the police.

For your file

Write a statement giving your views about carrying knives and saying what you think can be done to reduce the problem of knife crime.

You can give information about knives and knife crime anonymously by contacting Crimestoppers at www.crimestoppers-uk.org or on 0800 555 111.

In groups

Study the statements (above) about carrying knives. Discuss each one and say why you agree or disagree with it.

Talk about the suggested ways of cutting down on knife crime. Which do you think would be most effective? What other measures can you suggest?

Assertive, aggressive or passive

Everyone has to learn how to deal with difficult situations. Whatever situation you are faced with, there are three ways you can react. You can be either **assertive**, **aggressive** or **passive**.

Let's say that you've made an arrangement to meet a friend and they turn up half an hour late. There are three ways you could behave:

- You could get angry and shout at them. That's being **aggressive**.

- You could say nothing and bottle up your feelings, even though you're furious. That's being **passive**.

- Or you could calmly but tactfully tell them that you're feeling very fed up with them, because they've kept you waiting. That's being **assertive**.

Learning to be assertive will increase your self-esteem, because you can stand up for yourself and express how you feel. This will make you feel more confident in being able to deal with difficult situations.

If you are constantly being aggressive, people will think of you as rude and arrogant and are less likely to hear what you are trying to say. If your behaviour is passive, they may start to take advantage of you, thinking that you'll just do put up with anything.

In pairs

1 Study the article 'It doesn't pay to be passive'. What other reasons are there why people sometimes behave passively rather than assertively? What does Erica Stewart say are the consequences of behaving passively?

2 Discuss any situations in the past in which you have behaved passively and how you feel about having done so.

It doesn't pay to be
passive

Erica Stewart explains why people don't always assert themselves and what the consequences are.

When we're faced with a difficult situation, it can be easier to say nothing and do nothing, rather than to speak up and say what we really feel. But taking the easy way out can leave us feeling angry, disappointed and frustrated, so why do we do it?

There are two main reasons why we don't stand up for ourselves. First, there's a fear of failure, particularly if we're dealing with someone who is older than us or in a position of power or authority. What if we try to put our point of view, or to make a request, only for it to be brushed aside or dismissed?

The other reason we may choose not to say what we think or feel is because we're afraid there'll be a scene. We're anxious about how people will react, and worried that they'll get angry and take their anger out on us. Some people are very uncomfortable with confrontation and would rather avoid it.

The trouble is, if you don't do or say anything, nothing will change. You're left feeling upset and the situation may even get worse. If you don't tell people what's bothering you and why, you're not giving them the chance to do something about it. How can they know what you think if you don't say?

So it's far better to take a deep breath and say what you feel. At least you'll feel you tried, even if you don't seem to get anywhere. And that will also help to build your self-esteem.

Assertive, aggressive and passive behaviour

Assertive behaviour	Aggressive behaviour	Passive behaviour
You are prepared to ask for what you want.	You demand what you want.	You don't ask for what you want.
You express your feelings directly and openly.	You express your feelings loudly and rudely.	You do not express your feelings openly.
You behave calmly and politely.	You behave angrily and threateningly.	You behave submissively.
You stand up for your rights.	You tell people what your rights are.	You don't stick up for your rights.
You behave confidently.	You behave selfishly and arrogantly.	You lack confidence.
You acknowledge and respect other people's feelings.	You don't respect other people's feelings.	You are too mindful of other people's feelings and try to do nothing that will upset them.
You listen to and consider what other people say.	You don't acknowledge that other people may have their own viewpoints.	You take too much notice of what other people think and say.
You are willing to negotiate and compromise.	You are stubborn and unwilling to compromise.	You agree with anything in order to avoid confrontations.
When you want something, you explain why.	You tell people what you want, but you don't explain why.	You rely on others knowing what you want.

In pairs

Study the lists (above) and discuss the differences between assertive, aggressive and passive behaviour. Then study the 8 situations on the right. For each situation, write down what would be:

a) assertive behaviour,
b) aggressive behaviour, and
c) passive behaviour.

Then join up with another pair and compare your answers.

Role play

In pairs, choose one of the situations and role play it in three different ways to show the difference between an assertive, an aggressive and a passive response.

1 You lend a friend a DVD. She keeps on saying she's going to give it back, but she's now had it for a fortnight.

2 A group of friends have bought some alcohol. They offer you a drink, but you don't want one. They start to pressurise you to have one.

3 A teacher wants you to audition for a part in the school play. You are having trouble keeping up with your school work and don't really want to audition for the part.

4 Your parents want you to spend the weekend with their friends who have a teenager your age. But your interests are totally different and you know from past experiences that the two of you won't get on.

5 You are with a group of people and some of them start making racist remarks.

6 You are out with someone who suddenly starts taking things in a shop. They put one of the items in your bag.

7 You feel your boyfriend or girlfriend is becoming jealous and possessive, but you don't want to break off the relationship completely.

8 Your friend is very unhappy because he is going through a bad patch. He is biting his nails until they bleed and other people are making remarks about it.

How to be assertive

How to be assertive

Being assertive is about having the confidence and skills that enable you:

- **To express positive feelings.** For example, to give and receive compliments, to ask for help and make requests, to approach people and begin conversations, to show affection and to express appreciation.

- **To express negative feelings.** For example, to tell people you are feeling hurt and why, to show and explain justifiable annoyance.

- **To stand up for your rights.** For example, to refuse to be pressurised into doing something you don't want to do, to make complaints, to express personal opinions, to reject unfair criticism and put-downs.

To be assertive you need to know what you want to say and how to say it. You also need to choose the right moment to say it. If you don't choose the right moment, you may fail to get your message across. For example, if your mum is getting ready to go to a business meeting and is running late, it's hardly the best time to ask her for a pocket money rise.

Say 'no' and mean it

If you really don't want to do something, don't allow yourself to be pushed into doing it. Use your body language to help you to refuse. Stand up straight with your head up to show that you aren't afraid. If appropriate give an explanation, but don't get drawn into an argument. Don't apologise for refusing and don't allow any taunts to get to you. Just say no and keep repeating it until whoever it is accepts your decision or you move away from them. Remember that real friends will respect you more for being your own person and not bowing to pressure than they will if you give in and do something you didn't want to do.

Repeating the message

This is a technique that you can use if you feel someone isn't listening to you or is deliberately trying to lead the conversation in a different direction in order to refuse your request or ignore your point of view. You keep on repeating the same sentence or phrase over and over again so as to get your message across. It is particularly useful:

- when you want someone to recognise your right to feel the way you do

- when you want to refuse to do something

- when you are being denied your legal rights, for example, by a shop-keeper who is refusing to exchange faulty goods or to give you a refund.

For your file

Think of a difficult situation that you have had to deal with and write about how you handled it. Were you assertive? Did you handle it as well as you could have done? If you were to be in a similar situation again, what would you do differently?

Saying what you want – confidence tips

The snag is, once you've decided what you really want, you still have to get the message over to someone else. This is never easy. As a young person you may often feel lacking in power, but there are tricks to feeling more confident and to help you grasp some of the power and control for yourself.

Step 1: Decide what you want to say

Obviously when you tackle somebody about a difficult or sensitive problem there's going to be a lot of talk and probably a lot of emotion, but you should have in your mind one simple clear phrase or idea you want to get over.

Step 2: Get your message across

You also have to make sure that your message is delivered in a very direct way. You may not be feeling very good about yourself but you are sure about the idea you want to get across. Standing in a corner mumbling it at your shoes won't help anyone. Looking the other person in the face and saying it directly to them makes you look and sound self-assured and confident. Holding their gaze for just a few seconds will add a tremendous amount of power to your words.

Step 3: Keep it short, keep it simple

It's very tempting when you're feeling unsure of yourself to dress up your message in lots of meaningless words like: 'Well, I was just wondering, if you really don't mind, it's just that I thought perhaps it might be a good idea ...' These are all very nice things to say, but they aren't going to help. They also prolong the agony. So look the person in the eye and say what you have to say, clearly and simply.

Step 4: Acknowledge their feelings – but keep going back to the message

What you have to say is going to have some emotional effect on the other person. They may be surprised, shocked, angry or whatever, and start shouting at you or trying to argue with you. Stand firm. Acknowledge their feelings, for example, 'I know that you're upset about this, but ...' and then go back and repeat your message.

Step 5: Don't get angry

Try to keep the emotional temperature as normal as possible. If the other person starts getting angry or extremely upset, try saying, 'Please don't be angry, this is something we need to discuss.' Say it calmly and keep on saying it. If you really can't get anywhere, then tell them you'll just have to discuss it later when they are feeling more calm.

Role play

In pairs, develop a series of role plays in which you take it in turns to practise being assertive. Here are some possible situations:

1 You take some faulty goods back to a shop and ask the manager for a refund.

2 You ask your parents if you can go to stay with a friend who your parents don't particularly like.

3 A friend is pressurising you to do something you don't want to do.

In groups

1 Study the advice in the article (left). Which piece of advice is the most helpful?

2 Who is it easiest to be assertive with – your parents, your brothers and sisters, your friends, strangers?

Reviewing your strengths

Some teenagers have a clear idea of what job they would like to do. Many others have little or no idea of what they want to do in the future. Even if you think you know now, your ideas may change, so it's worth analysing your strengths to see what sorts of jobs may suit you.

One way of identifying your strengths is to think about your interests and personal qualities.

Your interests

You need to think about your out of school hobbies and activities as well as your school work. Many of you will have strengths and skills that you have developed by being a member of a club, or by accompanying an adult and sharing the experience of an activity they enjoy.

For example, Archie enjoys helping his dad on his allotment and is already a skilled gardener himself. Jason sometimes helps his uncle whose hobby is restoring old furniture. Priya's gran has taught her to sew and she enjoys making her own clothes. Tracey is always on the computer and is fascinated by programs that show her how to design things.

Your personal qualities

When you are thinking about careers, it is important to consider what your personal qualities are in order to see whether they match up to the personal qualities required for any job you are considering.

There is a wide variety of different personal qualities, for example:

adventurous   assertive   calm   careful
competent   concerned   conscientious   cooperative
curious   easy-going   enthusiastic   flexible
generous   good-tempered   hard-working   honest
humorous   imaginative   open-minded
patient   persevering   polite   punctual
questioning   reliable   resourceful   self-confident
sincere   sympathetic   tidy   tolerant.

In pairs

Discuss what your interests are. Are there any particular skills and strengths you have developed as a result? Suggest the sort of jobs in which you might be able to use those skills.

On your own, study the list of qualities (left) and decide which of them belong to you. Be honest and fair. Most people have a mixture of good and not-so-good qualities. List the qualities that you think are your strong points, then show your partner your list and discuss together why you picked out those qualities and what this tells you about your strengths and weaknesses.

Different types of work

Different types of work require different qualities and abilities. On the right are examples of qualities and abilities you need in certain types of work. In addition, there are a number of qualities that are required in all jobs, such as reliability, honesty, perseverance, the ability to keep your temper and a good sense of humour.

"I think that my main qualities are that I'm kind and considerate. I'm also patient and calm. I was able to cope when my nan had a stroke, while she was babysitting me and my younger brother, and I helped mum to look after her when she came to live with us afterwards. I'm not so adventurous though and I wouldn't want a job that involved a lot of travelling about. I think I'd like a job in care work of some kind – perhaps working in a care home for older people. I know the pay's not likely to be very good, but I don't mind that."

Orla (14)

ADMINISTRATIVE WORK

You need to be:
- an efficient organiser
- neat and methodical
- good at spelling and punctuation
- good with figures
- able to get on with people
- happy with a routine.

CREATIVE WORK

You need to be:
- imaginative and articulate
- artistic
- flexible
- happy working under pressure.

TECHNICAL AND SCIENTIFIC WORK

You need to be:
- interested in problem-solving
- able to work in a team
- practical and methodical
- good with numbers and calculations.

CARING WORK

You need to be:
- interested in people and their problems
- patient and understanding
- sympathetic but firm-minded
- able to remain calm in emergency situations.

CONSTRUCTION WORK

You need to be:
- happy working outdoors
- physically fit
- able to work as part of a team.

SERVICE WORK (SHOPS, CATERING ETC.)

You need to be:
- able to get on with people
- willing to be on your feet most of the time
- prepared to wear some sort of uniform
- good with figures
- honest and reliable.

In pairs

Study the qualities and abilities required for each area of work. Think about your own qualities and abilities. Discuss which area of work you think your qualities and abilities seem to match most closely. If you had to choose a job in one of these areas, which area would you choose and why?

Think about different areas of work, for example, agricultural work, medical work, media work, hotel work, legal work, financial services, police service. List the qualities and abilities that you need for that particular area of work.

For your file

Use the list you made of your own qualities to help you to write a statement about yourself similar to the statement Orla has written (above left). Show your statement to someone who knows you well – a parent, a teacher or a friend – and see if they agree that it is a true reflection of your personal qualities.

Finding information about careers

There are several ways of investigating careers, besides reading the books and pamphlets that are available in the library or resources centre.

The National Careers Service provides careers advice on a wide range of jobs, training courses, resources and funding https://nationalcareersservice.direct.gov.uk

It offers a free Skills Health Check and also has a telephone helpline 0800 100 900.

Arrange to visit a workplace

One of your parents, relatives or family friends may be able to arrange for you to visit their workplace, so that you can see for yourself what a particular job involves. Alternatively, if it is a large firm, you may be able to go on a conducted tour.

When you go on a visit, make full use of it by asking questions, writing down anything you need to remember and collecting any pamphlets or brochures that can give you further information.

For your file

Arrange to talk to someone who works in a career in which you are currently interested, to visit a workplace or to spend a day shadowing somebody at work.

After your visit, write a short statement to put in your file, saying what you learned from the experience.

Work shadowing
See if you can arrange to spend a day work shadowing.

Jamie's story

Jamie thought he might like to be a plumber. So when his Uncle Dave offered to let him spend a day seeing what it was like working as a plumber he gratefully accepted.

By the end of the day he'd learned a lot about what it involved. The first call they made took up most of the morning, which meant they were late for the second call. Even though his uncle phoned up to say they were held up, the customer was angry and rude. He was surprised by how many of the jobs weren't straightforward and involved solving problems, which he found interesting. But he wasn't prepared for how dirty some of the work was and how his uncle often had to crawl around in people's attics to get to their water tanks.

Although he knew his uncle made good money, he was no longer sure that he wanted to spend all the day working on his own in people's houses, doing things like unblocking sinks and replacing broken toilets. He now had a much clearer idea of what working as a plumber was like.

Talk to someone who is doing the job

You or your parents may already know someone who works in the career area which you are interested in. If so, do not be afraid to ask them about their job and the qualifications that are needed to do it.

To make full use of the opportunity of talking to someone, prepare for the conversation, as if you are planning to interview them. Draw up a list of the information you want to discover and the questions you want to ask.

If you do not know someone, then use your initiative. You could telephone or write to a local firm to see if there is someone in the firm who would be willing to spare some time to talk to you.

Researching different jobs

When you are researching different jobs, it is a good idea to have a list of questions that you want to ask and to record the information that you find out. Below is a Job factsheet that lists the questions that you may want answered by your research.

Job factsheet

Name of job.............................

....

Researched by ....

Date...

1. What particular activities does the job require you to do? (For example, answering the telephone, using a computer, handling money etc.)

2. What sort of place would you be working in? (For example, would you be working indoors or outdoors, in an office, out on a site, in a factory, a shop or somewhere else?)

3. Would you be working on your own or with others?

4. What are the particular qualities and skills you require for this job?

5. What qualifications do you require in order to do this job?

6. Where can you get the necessary training, education or experience for this job?

7. Are there any particular restrictions about this job? (For example, do you have to be over a certain age? Are there any medical restrictions, such as not being colour blind?)

8. What are the rewards of this job? (For example, high salary, flexible working hours, challenges, excitement, job satisfaction.)

9. What are the drawbacks of this job? (For example, shift work including night shifts, years of training, repetitive work, unchallenging.)

10. What is the career structure in this type of work? Are there plenty of opportunities for promotion?

11. What is the competition like for this type of job? Are there plenty of these jobs available or are there a lot of people competing for a few jobs?

12. Where are there opportunities for this type of job? (For example, only in large cities or in particular areas of the country where companies are located.)

Conclusion

Now that you have researched this job, what conclusion have you reached? Give the reasons why you think you would or would not consider doing this job as a career.

The influence of the press

Censorship of the press

Case study – North Korea

In North Korea, all radio, TV and newspaper reports are controlled by the government. All news is presented so that it shows the government in a positive light.

North Korea is reported to have an army of 1.21 million, the 4th largest in the world after China, the USA and India. The North Korean media reports that it is necessary to have so many troops because it needs to defend itself against South Korea and the USA, who are preparing an attack.

North Koreans are isolated from the rest of the world, and have an authoritarian leadership who controls information, denying them rights which citizens in other countries enjoy and ruthlessly repressing anyone who dares to challenge the 'facts' presented by the media.

The press in Britain

In Britain, as in other democracies, there is a free press. Newspapers and magazines are owned and run by private companies.

The largest company is News Corp International, run by Rupert Murdoch, which owns *The Times*, *The Sunday Times* and *The Sun*. Other owners include the Barclay brothers who own *The Telegraph Group* and the family of the Russian millionaire Alexander Lebedev, who own the *London Evening Standard* and *The Independent*.

However, even in a democracy such as Britain, there are some curbs on the power of the press. For example, the government exercises some control. During national emergencies it may censor reports. Also, the government will sometimes issue a D-notice, or defence notice, to newspaper editors, requesting them not to publish reports on certain subjects in the interests of national security.

There are a number of legal restrictions too, which limit what the press can publish, such as the libel laws, official secrets and anti-terrorism legislation and the laws of contempt and other restrictions on court reporting.

In groups

1 Is it right that people who are not UK citizens, such as Rupert Murdoch, a Australian/US citizen, and Alexander Lebedev, a Russian, should own British newspapers? Should anyone who owns a UK newspaper have to be British, live in Britain and be a UK taxpayer

2 Should there be a limit to how many papers a compan is allowed to own, for example, only two national newspapers? What are the reasons why some people argue that there should be a limit?

What controls the content of newspapers?

Newspaper owners, or proprietors, have tremendous power to influence the political message that their papers give. Traditionally, papers such as the *Daily Mail* and the *Daily Express* have supported the Conservative Party, while the *Daily Mirror* has supported the Labour Party. While the views of owners have a considerable influence on the content of newspapers, they are by no means the only factor. Another very important influence is consumer demand. Newspapers have to provide readers with what they want to read, otherwise they wouldn't sell enough copies. So a newspaper like the *Sun* contains lots of human interest stories and few international news stories, because that's what the readership wants.

Another commercial factor is the need to attract advertisers. The revenue from advertising is crucial to newspapers. So the stories they contain must attract the audience that their advertisers want. They must also be careful not to include stories that might offend the advertisers.

The editor and journalists of a newspaper also have to decide on how newsworthy a particular story is. The amount of space given to a report will depend on what the journalists consider to be the news value of the issue or topic.

News management

A lot of news comes from big businesses and government. They want newspapers to portray them in a positive light, so they use public relations specialists to help them in their dealings with the press.

Political parties have become increasingly skilful at what is known as 'spin doctoring': presenting their news in a way that makes their policies appear successful and gives them good publicity. They are also skilful at distracting attention from things they do not wish to receive too much media coverage. For example, they often time their press releases so that a positive story hits the headlines on the same day as a negative report is to be issued.

In groups

Study two or three different newspapers for the same day. What are the main stories in each paper? Compare the different amounts of space they give to particular stories. What do you learn about the news values of the different newspapers?

Press regulation

In 2011, it emerged that thousands of people had been the victims of press intrusion. Journalists had been hacking into the phones not only of celebrities, such as Steve Coogan and Charlotte Church, but of the murdered schoolgirl Milly Dowler, of the relatives of deceased soldiers and of victims of the 7/7 London bombings.

This led to the closure of the *News of the World* and a public inquiry into how the press is regulated, led by Lord Leveson. The Leveson inquiry recommended that newspapers should continue to be self-regulated and that the government should have no power over what they publish. A new press standards body should be created, backed by legislation to ensure that the body was independent and effective.

But newspapers opposed legislation, arguing that it would give politicians an 'unacceptable degree of interference'.

In groups

Are there any circumstances in which phone hacking by reporters can be justified? What methods of gaining information should newspapers be allowed to use and not be allowed to use? Should investigative journalists be able to use whatever means they like to uncover information that people would prefer to be kept secret?

Who has the right to decide what the public should know or not know? And how can they decide what is in the public interest?

Should the press be self-regulated? Should it be regulated by politicians? Should it be accountable to a public body and, if so, how should the members of that body be appointed?

Public interest versus private rights

Politicians, pop stars, princesses – the roles carried out by all these people means that they attract a great deal of media attention. Most of them thrive on it, but when journalists begin to ask questions about their private lives, they are usually less keen to be in the spotlight. When does media interest become an unacceptable invasion of privacy?

For some journalists, especially those working for the tabloid newspapers, the issue is a simple one:

'The acid test of whether a story should be published is simple: Is it true? If it is, and the truth hurts, that is no argument for suppression.' *The Sun.*

Diana, Princess of Wales, spent all her adult life in the glare of the media. Editors knew that they could increase circulation simply by putting a photograph of her on their front pages. When she was killed in a car crash in Paris in 1997 while trying to evade photographers, there was a strong public feeling that the media had killed her. There were calls for stronger laws to protect people's privacy but the key problem of balancing the right to privacy with the 'right to know' remains.

The issue becomes even more complicated when public figures try to have the best of both worlds, being paid by gossip magazines for photographs of their family wedding, for example, but complaining about media attention on other occasions. Is it reasonable to expect the media to take an interest in people's private lives only when it suits those involved?

In groups

"Celebrities shouldn't moan about the press. If you're a public figure, then you've just got to accept the fact that people are interested in you."

"People have a right to their privacy. There should be a privacy law to protect people from press harassment."

Discuss these views.

Teen magazines

What do you think of teen magazines?

Teen magazines are designed and written by adults. Are you reading what you actually want to read or are you reading what adults think you want to read?

What teenagers say:

"Teen magazines are patronising. They seem to think that all teenagers are interested in are pop stars, fashion, soaps and sex."

"All the magazines are for girls. Why aren't there any magazines for boys?"

"Teen magazines are entertaining and fun. I don't think they really have much influence on what we think."

"There should be more articles written by teenagers for teenagers about serious matters."

"Teen magazines exploit teenagers. They do the fashion and pop industries' advertising for them, encouraging us to want things we don't need and can't afford."

"You can learn a lot about life from teen magazines – from things like the problem pages and readers' true experiences."

What the editors and magazine journalists say:

"We're providing teenagers with what they want. If we didn't we'd go out of business because they wouldn't buy the magazines."

"There's plenty of opportunity for teenagers to have their say. We're always interviewing them and running articles based on readers' responses."

"Of course some of the articles are trivial, but so is a lot of life and it's our job to entertain, not educate."

"We don't create teen culture. That's done by TV and films and the pop business and the fashion industry. We have far less influence than they do."

"We're sometimes criticised for having too many articles about sex. But we provide teenagers with a lot of information that they wouldn't otherwise get."

"It's wrong to say there aren't any magazines for boys. There are lots of special interest magazines. Those are the ones boys buy."

In groups

1 Discuss the comments about teen magazines. Talk about their content. Do they provide what teenagers want? Are teen magazines patronising? Do they manipulate teenagers' tastes and fashions? How much influence do you think teenage magazines have?

2 Draft a proposal for a new teen magazine. Draw up full details of its contents and then present your ideas to the rest of the class.

Compare your ideas for new magazines with the magazines that are currently produced for teenagers. In what ways are your magazines different? How does your view – the teenager's own view – of what teenagers want to read differ from the adult's view?

For your file

Make a detailed study of a teen magazine. Analyse its content, working out how much space is devoted to particular features, for example, fiction, pop, sport, hobbies, letters, social issues etc. Draw a pie-chart showing how the content of your magazine is divided. Write a few sentences saying what you have learned from your study about what the magazine editors think teenagers are interested in.

Eating disorders — anorexia

Anorexia nervosa

What is anorexia?

Anorexia nervosa is an eating disorder, often described as the 'slimmer's disease'. While the name means nervous loss of appetite, this is misleading. Sufferers of anorexia have not lost their appetite, but have lost the ability to let themselves eat food. They think about food, how they can resist eating and the way their body looks. Doctors define someone as anorexic when they have lost at least 15% of their normal weight, have a fear of fatness and think they look fatter than they really are. Anorexia is not a diet gone wrong. Anorexic people are sufferers of a serious mental health problem.

Who suffers from anorexia?

Over 700,000 people in Britain suffer from the disease. Anorexia most often occurs during adolescence in girls aged 12 to 17. But 1 in 10 sufferers is a boy. Boys are more likely to become obsessed with exercising than girls, and boy sufferers may spend every moment of the day exercising to burn off calories.

Is there a cure?

There is no pill that cures anorexia. Feeding someone with anorexia until they are of normal weight does not work. If this happens the sufferer will just go away and stop eating again because the original problems have not been solved.

In order to recover, people with anorexia need to accept and like themselves, and they need to work on the problems that have caused their illness. It is difficult for sufferers to get better on their own. They need help from a doctor or from an organisation called BEAT (see details, below).

Some sufferers may need to go into hospital for a while, and they will need support from their family and friends. The sooner a person gets help, the quicker their recovery will be.

> More information and advice can be obtained from:
> BEAT: beating eating disorders at www.b-eat.co.uk
> Contact the BEAT youth helpline on 0845 634 7650

PORTIA'S STORY

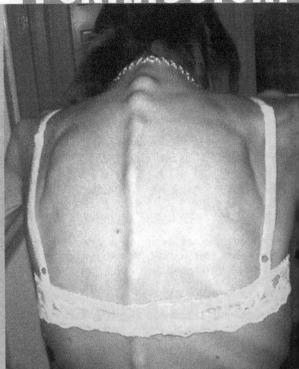

Portia's problems began around the age of 12 when she joined her sister at a weekly boarding school.

'I was homesick and unhappy from the start. I am naturally shy and self-conscious and did not keep up socially.' She was clever, though, and threw herself obsessively into academic achievement.

To the growing anxiety of her parents, she began to eat less and less. 'I rallied for a while, especially during holidays. Deep down, I think I knew what was happening, but could not relate it to myself. Working hard and not eating were distractions from feeling unhappy.' To her teachers, her academic success was welcome. However, there was little supervision of meals, so no one noticed her increasing absences.

'My condition is like an addiction and television and magazines somehow reinforce it. To me, not eating is a way of controlling the real world, which is too intense to manage. So many people seem to think you are being selfish.' Almost tearful, she insists: 'It is not deliberate.'

eating disorders

What causes an eating disorder?

There are no simple answers to what causes an eating disorder. In most cases it's a combination of different factors which cause a person to become ill. What is known is that some people are more vulnerable to eating disorders than others.

Perfectionism

Perfectionists – or rather, people who have unrealistic expectations of themselves and others – are more prone to becoming ill. This is because people like this feel inadequate and worthless no matter what they achieve. Everything in their lives becomes about 'being better' and often the pursuit of thinness is a part of this.

Control

Other people have eating disorders because they want to avoid something painful in their lives – perhaps a family problem or sexuality. Becoming locked in the behaviour patterns of a disorder helps them to bring an element of control to their lives.

Family triggers

Some people's families are overprotective and sometimes rigid in the way they deal with problems and conflict. When this occurs some people try to resolve their problems through what they do and don't eat.

Media pressure

Because of the media attention on women's bodies and strict cultural ideas equating thinness with female attractiveness, girls have been greatly affected by eating disorders. Increasingly, male bodies also suffer from harsh media scrutiny, where the emphasis is usually more on appearing to be big or 'strong'.

External problems

Sometimes, external change can trigger an eating disorder. For instance, bullying, sexual abuse, the break-up of a relationship or moving home.

The red flags of an eating disorder

- A desperate preoccupation with weight, shape, food, calories and dieting.
- Overly and negatively fixating on looks.
- Imagining problems would be solved by being thin.
- An excessive and rigid exercise regime.
- Avoiding situations when food is present.
- Letting food and eating overshadow everything you do.
- Desire to eat alone.

MARK'S STORY

I didn't suddenly stop eating, it just crept up on me. I was always quite podgy in junior school and the other kids used to make fun of me because I couldn't run very fast. I was always one of the last to get picked for any team in games.

I had a stomach bug and lost a bit of weight while I was sick. I was rather pleased, so I decided to eat a bit less. I didn't bother much with dinner and my mum did evening classes and was always in such a rush, so she didn't really notice whether I ate tea.

I hoped that if I was thinner, I would be better at games and have more friends. But the other kids still made fun of me, because my legs got extremely thin.

My teacher phoned my mum about my weight and she took me to the doctor. I've seen loads of specialists and, when I got very thin, they put me in hospital. They tried to frighten me into eating by telling me I would die. In the end, I agreed to eat more so that I could come home. But as soon as I started putting on weight, I panicked and went back to not eating. I have dreadful rows with my dad about it, and he blames my mum. I just wish they'd leave me alone. It's my body.

In groups

1 Discuss Portia's story and Mark's story. What triggered them to become anorexics? What do you learn from their stories about what it feels like to be anorexic and how anorexia has affected their lives?

2 Talk about the various different factors that may cause a person to develop an eating disorder. What do you think are the main reasons why people become anorexic?

3 Discuss how helping a person with anorexia involves not only getting them to eat enough food to stay healthy but sorting out the problem that caused them to become anorexic.

Bulimia

What is bulimia?

Bulimia is an eating disorder that involves eating large amounts of food in a short period of time, then trying to get rid of it, for example, by vomiting it up.

Bulimics are often scared of the idea of gaining weight and will try to avoid food. Then, when the craving gets too much, they have a huge binge and try to get rid of the food afterwards by being sick, or taking laxatives which make them go to the toilet.

Bulimia can be a very difficult problem to spot. Bulimics often stay at a fairly normal weight and will eat quite sensibly and happily in front of friends and family. It's only in secret that they binge on all their 'forbidden treats' and then make themselves sick.

Even though people with bulimia don't usually starve themselves as sufferers of anorexia do, they're still putting their health at risk. Over time, being sick so often will damage the sufferer's teeth and gums and could cause mouth ulcers and throat infections. By getting rid of food quickly after eating, the sufferer's body doesn't have time to absorb vitamins and minerals from the food it's given, and eventually body organs like the kidneys and heart can be damaged.

Just as important, though, is what damage bulimia does to the sufferer's happiness. They feel guilty and exhausted from hiding their secret and end up hating themselves more than ever.

What causes bulimia?

Bulimia begins because the person feels deeply unhappy inside. Usually they have a low opinion of themselves, feel a failure, or set themselves impossibly high standards that they feel they can't live up to. They hide their problems because they feel that admitting to them would be like admitting they're 'not good enough'.

Bulimic people are nearly, but not always, female, and most often in their teens or early twenties. Often sufferers feel under pressure – maybe to do well at school, or to look a certain way, or from other problems.

When bulimics have a big food binge it isn't because they're greedy, and when they get rid of food by being sick or going to the loo, it isn't necessarily because they want to be thin.

Eating disorders are about using food to be in control. Teenagers face a lot of stress from exams, parents, friends, and just growing up in general, but often feel they have no power over their own lives. Sufferers may have been bullied or abused and made to feel powerless that way. They might decide without realising what they're doing that by making themselves sick they have some kind of control over their body.

What to do if a friend has bulimia

Don't accuse them

Just be there for them and make sure they know they can tell you anything and you won't judge them. Bulimics are very often people who desperately want to be perfect, so it can be hard for them to own up to having a problem. If they do confide in you, don't feel you have to give her lots of advice – just listen.

Be patient

Hard though it is, you can't make them get help. That's got to be their decision. You can find information from internet sites and groups like

Beat (the Eating Disorders Association) to encourage them, but the rest is up to them.

Be positive

Bulimics already spend most of their time worrying about food, so try to show there's more to life. Don't discuss the problem as if that's the most important thing about them – get them out there and have fun, so they can feel like a normal person. You may find they're moody and irritable sometimes (through lack of a healthy balanced diet) so try to be understanding.

In groups

Discuss what you learn from this page about what bulimia is, what causes it and what you can do to help a friend who is suffering from it.

Eating disorders and the media

Is there too much pressure to be thin?

Three young people express their views on how much pressure they feel the media puts on teenagers to be thin.

"I think there's an over-reaction to the effect that skinny models have on girls. We're not mindless idiots sucked in by every image fed to us. There are many other influences at work including peer-group pressure.

When I see beautiful celebrities, of course I think it would be lovely to look like them, but I'm over the fact that I don't match up to supermodels. I know now that magazines show impossibly perfect models in photos that have been touched up – a practice I feel should be banned." Anna Rose Sheppard, 19

"When it comes to pointing the finger, I don't think the media should shoulder all the responsibility. Friends and family are a bigger influence – and usually dieting is a sign of a problem more deep-rooted than just thinking you don't possess the perfect vital statistics." Lavon Hendricks, 16

There's pressure on boys too. Whereas the pressure on girls is about being very thin, for boys it's to be muscular and lean, fitting the image that is presented as being manly and attractive in magazines and movies.

Studies show that 30% of adolescent men are concerned about their weight and this can lead to crash diets and over-exercising.

In groups

1 Do you think there is too much media pressure on girls to be thin and to look like supermodels? Say why you agree or disagree with the views expressed by the three teenagers (right).

Does the media put pressure on boys to look athletic and to conform to a certain body shape?

2 "The secret of being a truly attractive person has nothing to do with your dimensions. Intelligence, personality, confidence and social skills all count far more when it comes to being a happy and therefore an attractive person." – Adele Lovell

Discuss Adele Lovell's view. How far is attractiveness what a person looks like? How much does it depend on a person's character and how they behave?

For your file

Write a statement saying how much pressure you think media images put on young people and which you think is more important – personality or looks.

Understanding qualifications and courses

The options you choose for Years 10 and 11 will affect how you spend your time at school for the next two years. The choices you make may also influence what course or job you decide to do after Year 11.

Some people think that making these choices is a bit scary, but it is actually your opportunity to take control of your education and shape the way you want your future to be. It is also your chance to start laying foundations for what you do after Year 11.

Different schools offer different options, and different options lead to different qualifications. So, before you decide what options to take, make sure you know what qualifications you will get and how they will help you in the future.

GCSE

This stands for General Certificate of Secondary Education. You can do GCSEs in many different subjects, including some with a work-related focus. GCSEs have a mix of theoretical study and investigative work. There are different types of GCSE courses including:

- GCSE – one full GCSE, often called a single award.
- Short course GCSE – often called a half GCSE because it covers half the material of a full GCSE.
- Double award GCSE – the equivalent of two full GCSEs.

GCSE assessment is through a mix of written examinations and internal assessment.

Entry Level Certificate

You can do Entry Level Certificates in National Curriculum subjects, vocational subjects and the skills you need for work and life. They are assessed through tests, coursework and a portfolio of evidence that shows what you have achieved.

NVQ

This stands for National Vocational Qualification. It is a work-related qualification that develops the practical skills and knowledge needed in a specific job in a specific industry. In Years 10 and 11 you will usually work towards NVQs at Level 1 and/or Level 2. Assessment is through the observation of practical work and the creation of a portfolio of evidence.

VRQ

This stands for Vocationally Related Qualification. It is a work-related qualification that develops the skills and knowledge needed in a specific vocational area, such as information technology, sales or agriculture. Some courses last a few weeks, others take around the same time to do as four or five GCSEs. Assessment is generally through a mix of examinations, observation and the creation of a portfolio of evidence.

The Diploma

This is a new qualification based around a different style of teaching and learning. There are Diplomas in Engineering, Hair and Beauty Studies, Manufacturing and Product Design and many other areas. The Diploma combines classroom learning with practical hands-on experience, including the chance to spend at least 10 days working with an employer. All Diploma students complete a project to demonstrate the knowledge and skills that they have gained. In Years 10 and 11, Diplomas are available at two levels:

- a **Foundation Diploma** – a Level 1 qualification that is the equivalent of five GCSEs
- a **Higher Diploma** – a Level 2 qualification that is the equivalent of 5–6 GCSEs.

Young Apprenticeship

Young Apprenticeships combine classroom learning with practical learning. As well as studying the normal school curriculum, you spend 50 days gaining experience of work with an employer, training provider or college. You also work towards Level 2 work-related qualifications such as NVQs. Assessment includes written examinations, observation by an assessor and the creation of a portfolio of evidence.

For your file

Find out what courses your school offers by speaking to your careers co-ordinator and/or your Connexions personal adviser. Then write a personal statement describing what choices attract you after Year 9. Give reasons for your statements.

In groups

Discuss what you have learned about some of the different options that are available at the end of Year 9.

Draw up a list of advantages of each of the main options described here. What disadvantages are there?

Choosing GCSE courses

GCSE courses last two years. They usually combine coursework with a final exam at the end. GCSEs are a good course to take because they are recognised by many different employers.

To find out what the different subjects might cover, look at the information about GCSE courses on these pages.

In pairs

List the sorts of things that you enjoy doing, in all areas of life. What keeps you interested? What makes you work hard? If you have any career ideas and interests, note these too.

With a partner, discuss which subjects you would like to do. How do these match your interests or career choices?

Compulsory subjects

These are the subjects that everyone must study in Years 10 and 11 because they are important for work and for adult life. Everyone takes a 'core' group of subjects: English, mathematics and science. In addition, there are other compulsory 'foundation' subjects:

- **Information and Communication Technology (ICT)**
- **Citizenship**
- **Physical Education (PE)**
- **Religious studies**
- **Sex and Relationship Education.**

All schools have to offer these subjects, but they can decide whether the course ends with a qualification.

ENGLISH

What's involved? Reading different types of texts, writing for different purposes and audiences, speaking and listening, expressing your views and presenting arguments.

Career ideas: Social scientist, journalist, librarian, market researcher, public relations officer, publishing editor, solicitor, teacher, author.

MATHEMATICS

What's involved? Using numbers, algebra, measurement, shapes and space. Learning about handling money, working with statistics and using numerical information to solve real-life problems.

Career ideas: Accountant, bank/building society adviser, engineer, financial adviser/analyst.

SCIENCE

What's involved? Understanding and describing the world about you and exploring how science affects your everyday life. You may be able to study biology (living things), chemistry (the study of the structure of substances and how they react with other substances), and physics (the study of forces such as heat, light and sound and the way in which they effect objects) as separate sciences or take a science or applied science course that combines all three.

Career ideas: Architect, doctor, beauty therapist, biochemist, chemist, conservation officer, dietitian, forensic scientist, healthcare assistant, marine biologist, pharmacist, research scientist, doctor, ecologist, veterinary nurse.

Optional subjects

Read your options information carefully as some schools make these subjects compulsory too.

ART AND DESIGN

What's involved? Using different materials and working in different media to develop your creative skills.
Career ideas: Animator, designer, fine artist, florist, jeweller, photographer, sculptor.

BUSINESS STUDIES

What's involved? Learning about the way companies are organised and run, national and international competition and e-commerce.
Career ideas: Administrator, business analyst, human resources officer, manager, payroll clerk, self-employment.

CITIZENSHIP STUDIES

What's involved? Learning about your role as a citizen in different local, national and international communities, including how to change things for the better.
Career ideas: Fundraiser, journalist, occupational psychologist, police officer, social worker.

DESIGN AND TECHNOLOGY

What's involved? Creative and practical work with different tools and materials. Using planning, designing, making and evaluation skills.
Career ideas: Architect, carpenter/joiner, graphic designer, model maker, product designer, shopfitter.

DRAMA

What's involved? Learning about production techniques and how to stage performances, including backstage operations, lighting, costume, set design and make-up.
Career ideas: Actor, director/producer, lighting technician, stage manager, wardrobe assistant.

ECONOMICS

What's involved? Learning about the production and distribution of income and wealth and how consumers, producers and governments behave when managing scarce resources.
Career ideas: Accountant, auditor, credit analyst, economic development officer, investment analyst.

ENGINEERING

What's involved? Learning about engineering products, systems and services and working with design briefs.
Career ideas: Electrical engineer, materials technician, mechanical engineer, production engineer, telecommunications technician.

GEOGRAPHY

What's involved? Learning about landscapes and climates, population and land use, and how humans interact with and affect the environment.
Career ideas: Conservation officer, geologist, surveyor, town planner, transport planner.

HEALTH AND SOCIAL CARE

What's involved? Learning about the care that people of all ages need and how service providers meet these needs. Exploring how to promote people's health and well-being.
Career ideas: Dental hygienist, dietitian, nurse, playworker, social care worker, social worker.

HISTORY

What's involved? Learning about the past and how different parts of the world have become the way they are today. Using different sources such as newspapers and artefacts to investigate the past.
Career ideas: Archaeologist, conservator, museum attendant, researcher, tourist guide.

INFORMATION AND COMMUNICATION TECHNOLOGY (ICT)

What's involved? Learning how information and communication systems work, how to store information and help people to solve problems. Exploring new developments in technology and different ways to use ICT.
Career ideas: Computer games designer, computer programmer, network manager, systems analyst, technical support person.

LEISURE AND TOURISM

What's involved? Learning about the leisure, tourism and travel industries. Developing practical skills in customer service, marketing and solving workplace problems.
Career ideas: Airline cabin crew, holiday representative, hotel receptionist, marketing manager, travel centre adviser.

MANUFACTURING

What's involved? Learning about the manufacturing industry including how products are designed and made, and the materials and technology used. Developing practical skills by designing and manufacturing a product.
Career ideas: Electronics assembler, manufacturing production manager, materials technician, product designer, quality control inspector.

MODERN FOREIGN LANGUAGES

What's involved? Reading, writing, speaking and listening in a foreign language, and developing an understanding of grammar and vocabulary. Most schools offer French, German and Spanish and many offer other languages.
Career ideas: Air traffic controller, EU official, importer/exporter, tourist guide, translator.

MUSIC

What's involved? Developing the knowledge, understanding and skills to perform, compose and appreciate all types of music.
Career ideas: DJ, composer, music therapist, musician, teacher.

PHYSICAL EDUCATION (PE)

What's involved? Doing physical activities, taking on different roles such as player and official, and learning how to assess your own and other people's performance. Exploring how physical activity helps to maintain a healthy, balanced lifestyle.
Career ideas: Leisure centre assistant, physiotherapist, Royal Navy/Marine officer, sports coach, sports development officer.

PSYCHOLOGY

What's involved? Learning about the theories, concepts and research methods that are used to understand and explain human thoughts, emotions and behaviour. Exploring topical psychological issues that affect everyday life and the future of the world.
Career ideas: Counsellor, dramatherapist, educational psychologist, education welfare officer, forensic psychologist, image consultant.

Choosing GCSE courses

The new 14–19 curriculum gives you a choice of different routes and pathways. You will be able to mix and match different types of courses so that you end up with a Year 10 and 11 programme that suits you.

Choosing an option

■ Look at all your options before you make a decision.

■ Don't fall into the trap of thinking that some subjects are only for boys and some only for girls – this is not true.

■ If you have a firm career idea, choose subjects that you will need for the next stage of your career journey – those you need to go into further or higher education or into an apprenticeship or job with training.

■ If you don't have a firm career idea, choose subjects that will allow you to keep your options open.

DO choose a course because:

■ you are good at and think you will enjoy the subject

■ it links to a career idea

■ it will help you develop knowledge and skills that interest you

■ it will keep your options open in the future

■ you think that you might want to continue studying it after Year 11.

DO NOT choose a course because:

■ your friends have chosen it

■ you think it will be easy

■ someone else thinks that it is a good idea

■ you like the teacher you have now

■ you didn't have time to research your options properly.

Case study: Chris

Chris is in Year 10 and studying GCSE English, mathematics, science, ICT, religious studies, history, business studies and a Level 1 Certificate in Motor Vehicle Studies. Chris is currently unsure about his future career path.

Looking back on his Year 9 option choices, Chris found that talking to a range of people and asking their advice helped with the decision making. 'I talked to my Connexions personal adviser in school and also went to the options evening, where I got the chance to talk to my teachers about what subjects might be good for me.'

Chris also spoke to his family about which subjects they thought he would enjoy at school. This way, he gathered a range of information before finalising his decisions. 'Ultimately, I chose my Year 9 options based on what I am best at and what I am interested in. Even though I don't know what I want to do eventually as a career, I'm planning to stay in the school Sixth Form and continue my studies so that I can keep all my options open.'

For your file

Write a statement listing the options you have chosen and explaining why you have chosen them.

Getting help and support

Everyone needs a bit of help with decision-making. Your choices are too important to leave to chance so make sure that you get all the help and support you need.

Who knows you really well?

Share your ideas with someone you know and trust. They will soon tell you if they think that an option will suit you, and why. For example, could you talk to your parents and carers, other members of the family, friends, form tutor, subject teachers or learning support staff?

Who knows what you need to know?

Find out what courses are really like so that the learning activities, workload and assessment do not come as a surprise. Go to options events. Read the information you get. Talk to the people running the courses and the students who are doing them.

Who can give you practical help if you have trouble deciding which options to choose?

Get expert help if you can't decide what to do or if you want a second opinion from someone neutral.

- Have a chat with your **careers co-ordinator** – the person in charge of careers work in your school. Careers co-ordinators know a lot about what each option involves and how it might help you in the future. They can also tell you where to get more information and help.
- Ask to speak to a **Connexions personal adviser**. Connexions personal advisers are specially trained to help you sort out personal and career issues. Get in touch with an adviser through your form tutor. **National Careers Service advisers** are specially trained to help you sort out personal and career problems. You can talk to them online, **http://www.connexions-tw.co.uk/your-choices/**, on the phone **0800 100 900** and via e-mail, text and textphone.

Case study: Sarah-Jane

Sarah-Jane is 18. She says 'starting a college course at 14 has been the making of me.'

At the end of year 9, I was given the option of going to college one day a week to do a vocational course. I was given a variety of choices, including motor mechanics, animal care and health and beauty, but none of those appealed. My dad works in construction, and that had always interested me, so I thought I'd try a diploma in construction.

We had an hour-long lecture and two hours of practical work each week. Over a two-year period I covered a variety of areas, including plumbing, tiling, painting and decorating and bricklaying. I enjoyed tiling the most and found bricklaying the most challenging – it's a lot more complicated than it looks!

At school I always felt 'lost in the crowd', but at college I felt very supported. All the lecturers had current or recent industry experience, so I felt I was getting top-quality tuition.

Back at school, I grew in confidence. I stopped worrying and started asking for help when I needed it.

I achieved a distinction in the diploma and am now studying at Highbury College, Portsmouth for a national diploma in construction.

If I hadn't started college at 14, I'm not sure I'd have had this focus.

In groups

Read the case studies. What do you learn about
a) how Chris and Sarah-Jane made their decisions,
b) how the options they chose related to their skills and interests.

Youth courts

Youth courts

If you are aged between 10 and 17 years old and are charged with committing an offence, you will be tried in a youth court.

If you are 16 or under, a parent, guardian or social worker must attend the court with you. It is also advisable to consider getting a solicitor to speak for you in court.

The youth court is less formal than a magistrate's court. You will be tried by a panel of three magistrates and a legal clerk. They will listen to all the evidence, then state whether they find you guilty or not guilty.

It is important to try to make a good impression in court, so dress smartly and be polite. Don't put your hands in your pockets, don't chew gum and don't interrupt when other people are speaking. Don't be afraid to ask if you don't understand anything.

Youth Offending Teams

Youth offending teams work with young people who are in trouble with the law. They will get involved if:

- you are arrested or get into trouble with the police

- you are charged with an offence and have to go to court

- you are found guilty and given a sentence by the court.

They are separate from the police and the court. They will look into your background and try to help you stay out of trouble in the future.

What sentences can a youth court give?

The court may give a non-custodial sentence.

- You may be given a conditional discharge. Provided you do not reoffend within a set period of time, usually 1–2 years, you will not receive any punishment. But if you do reoffend, the court will take the original offence into consideration when sentencing you.

- You may be given a financial penalty, such as a fine or compensation order. If you are under 16 and have no money of your own, your parents will be responsible for payment.

- You may be given an attendance centre order of between 12 and 36 hours. This usually involves reporting to the centre for 2 hours a week on alternate Saturdays and doing various activities, including sports.

- You may be given a reparation order, which involves doing some work of benefit to your victim or the community, such as apologising or repairing damaged property.

- If you are aged 16–17, you may be given a curfew order. You are fitted with an electronic tag and are not allowed to be out at certain times. Electronic tags can also be used to keep an offender away from certain areas or buildings.

- You may be given a supervision order of between 6 months and 3 years, during which a member of the Youth Offending team will advise and support you. If you fail to co-operate, you can be taken back to court for re-sentencing.

In groups

"The time it takes for convictions to be spent is too long."

"Criminal records act as a deterrent."

"You are being punished twice. First, you lose your liberty, then you can't get a job because of your record. No wonder so many people reoffend."

Discuss these views.

Detention and training orders

A young person who repeatedly commits crimes or is found guilty of a serious offence may receive a detention and training order (DTO) of between four months and 24 months. A DTO is served in two parts – the first half of the sentence is served in custody. the second is served under supervision in the community.

If you receive a custodial sentence you will serve it in either a youth offending institution (for 15–21 year olds), a secure training centre (for 15–17 year olds) or a secure children's home (for 10–14 year olds).

In groups

Which sentences do you think are most effective and most likely to stop young people from reoffending?

Criminal records

A criminal record is held on a police database and contains details of any crimes you have been found guilty of or have admitted doing, and of any sentences you have been given.

If you admit to having committed a crime, the police may give you a warning or reprimand. These are not convictions and do not have to be declared, but are recorded on the police database.

You may be asked to declare whether or not you have a criminal record, when you apply for a job or to rent a flat. But after a certain time, your conviction becomes 'spent' and you no longer have to declare it.

For example, if you are under 18 and you receive a court fine or community sentence, it becomes spent after two and a half years. If you receive a custodial sentence of six months or less it becomes spent in three and a half years. Prison sentences of between six months and 30 months are spent after five years, but any longer prison sentences are never spent.

What's it like being in custody?

You are searched when you arrive and given prison clothes to wear. You are out of your room for most of the day. You have lessons that aim to equip you with the skills needed for a job or to enable you to return to education. You will take part in programmes to try to change and improve your behaviour and in sports and other activities.

"I was scared of what might happen to me, but I didn't really think about the consequences until I actually got sent down for six months. It was a big shock to me."

"Young offenders' institutes are worse than adult prisons because everybody there wants to be the 'top bloke' and there's lots of fighting and bullying."

"I found it really difficult. You have to portray yourself in a certain way in order to survive. You have to be a fighter and you have to be one of the mouthy ones who can handle themselves. Otherwise you just get picked on."

Matt

I had to learn the hard way

"If I was in school now and I was helping a young person with their problems, if I saw they were on the same path I went down, I would be warning them of everything that I've gone through with all the hardships and the family let-downs. I would make sure that they are aware of that so that they at least have the choice to change and they know what's going to happen."

"I spent six months thinking this was the world's fault. By the time I came out my perspective had changed. I saw the expressions on my family's faces. The first time my mum came to visit me in custody, I saw her expression, I had to learn the hard way that I had to do it all for myself."

Ryan

Over 70% of young people released from Young Offenders Institutions reoffend within a year.

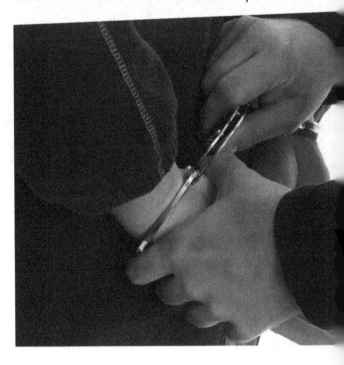

In groups

Research what is done to help young people who are released from youth custody to settle back into the community.

Then, imagine you work for an organisation such as NACRO (National Association for the Care and Resettlement of Offenders). A benefactor has left £20 million in their Will to be spent on keeping young offenders from re-offending. Discuss how you would spend the money.

How can crime be reduced?

The high level of crime is one of the major problems facing society. This page examines some of the ways that have been suggested of treating young offenders to cut down the amount of youth crime.

Naming and shaming young offenders

Youth courts now have the power to name persistent teenage offenders, who would previously have had their identities protected. They have been given such powers in the hope that naming and shaming young people will deter them from re-offending.

However, the courts have so far used these powers in a very limited way. Many people are concerned that publishing the names of young offenders may seriously damage efforts to rehabilitate or reform them, by giving them a bad name. Others feel that having their names made public only gives persistent young offenders the wrong sort of notoriety.

Tough sentences

Opinions are divided on the effectiveness of giving young offenders a custodial sentence in a detention centre with a strict regime. Some people think that giving young offenders a short, sharp shock will deter them from committing further offences. Others argue that such treatment does not have the desired effect and that there is no evidence that it actually reduces the number who reoffend.

Making young criminals face their victims

Making young criminals meet their victims face-to-face, apologise to them and make some form of reparation has helped to cut crime in some regions.

The young offender, their parents and victims who are willing to take part are brought together in a meeting at which the consequences of the crime are discussed and the offender is made to apologise. If appropriate, the young offender may be made to pay back the victim in some way, for example, by repairing the damage they caused.

24-hour monitoring

In the USA, schemes to monitor persistent offenders round the clock have cut crime.

Intensive Supervision and Surveillance Programmes (ISSP) have been introduced throughout England and Wales.

Supervision involves a minimum of 25 hours contact during the week with support in the evenings and at weekends.

Surveillance involves a mixture of tracking (regular contact), tagging (electronic monitoring) and voice verification (the offender's 'voice print' is used to check by telephone that they are where they should be).

In groups

Discuss these ways of dealing with young offenders. Which do you think is the most likely to be effective in reducing crime? Do you have any other suggestions on how to treat young offenders in order to reduce crime?

Communism (left-wing)	Centre	Fascism (right-wing)

Vladimir Lenin was a Russian communist revolutionary and politician

Adolf Hitler was the fascist dictator of Nazi Germany

Political parties and the political spectrum

A political party is a group of people who broadly share the same views about how a country should be governed. When we discuss the beliefs and policies of a political party we are discussing the party's political **ideology** – its ideas about the best kind of society to live in and how this can be achieved.

Political ideologies range from left-wing to right-wing. In general, left-wing parties are radical parties. This means they desire social and political change. Right-wing parties are usually conservative parties. They support traditional ideas and the retention of the existing social and political norms.

When we compare the ideologies of parties, we place them on what we call a political spectrum. The political spectrum is a line that extends from extreme left to extreme right.

Communism

The most extreme left-wing ideology is communism. It is regarded as a radical ideology because it aims to place all parts of the economy – the production and distribution of goods and services, and all financial institutions like banks – under the ownership and control of the state. There is little or no private ownership under communist rule.

Socialism

In a socialist system, there is some private ownership of small businesses, but banks, transport and communication facilities, and the supply of power, health and education services are owned and operated by the government. It is claimed that this type of social and economic system protects the workers from being exploited by unscrupulous employers.

Liberalism

Liberalism stresses the importance of the individual. Each individual has the right to lead his or her own life free from government restraints and control. Liberalism, therefore, argues that governments should not play a major role in the economy and should not interfere in society. Each individual should have the right, for example, to work as an employee without having to join a union, and to decide what he or she will watch or read without fear of government censorship.

Conservatism

Conservatives believe in the strength of tradition. They are reluctant to change society. They therefore support the existing situation or the status quo.

Fascism

Fascism is an extreme right-wing ideology. It demands the absolute loyalty and obedience of all citizens to the dictator and the political party the dictator leads. Fascism champions capitalism, bans organisations like trade unions, identifies other races and peoples as inferior, and stresses the importance of the state or nation that will endure for centuries.

In groups

1 What is meant by the political spectrum?

2 What is the difference between left-wing parties and right-wing parties?

3 What are the main ideas and beliefs of communism, socialism, liberalism and conservatism?

4 What is fascism? Why do the vast majorit of people find fascism repugnant?

The three main political parties in Britain

This page gives details of the three main parties.

Party ideologies

Labour Party

The Labour Party believes the government should work with private companies to provide good quality public services.

There needs to be different levels of tax depending on how much you earn. The more you earn, the more you should pay; otherwise you end up with a group of very, very rich people and very, very poor people. The tax is used to provide services for everybody, rich and poor.

Communities need to be strong by promoting tolerance of and respect for all by all. Everyone should enjoy their individual rights, but they must understand that they have responsibilities to those around them.

Labour believes that Britain has a very important part to play in Europe and should take a leading role, but has postponed joining the single currency until the time is considered right.

It has investigated electoral reform, but is not committed to it.

Conservative Party

The Conservative Party thinks that individuals should own and control businesses and services and make profits from them; the government should keep interference with these things to a minimum.

Tax should be low, so that you can keep as much of what you earn as possible. As businesses and services are privately owned, it's thought that people will have more money to spend on these things, instead of the government taking your money and choosing for you. In turn this will improve public services, because in order to get you to use them, they need to be good.

Traditional values should be encouraged to build strong communities and families. Strict discipline and respect will cut crime and criminals should be treated harshly.

It is against closer ties with Europe and against joining the single currency 'for the foreseeable future'.

The party is firmly against electoral reform.

The Liberal Democrats

The Liberal Democrats believe in personal freedom and a fair and open society where there is equality for everyone and strong communities. This can be achieved through free health care and education for all and by encouraging business to flourish by not interfering.

Tax should be set at a level whereby the poor and those in need could receive adequate help from the government.

They think it's more important to deal with the causes of crime not just the effects, otherwise it can never be reduced.

They support further development of the European Community.

They support full electoral reform and the introduction of proportional representation.

Study the list of key ideologies of the three main parties. Which of their policies do you most support? Why?

Other political parties

Scottish and Welsh Nationalist parties

The Scottish Nationalist Party campaigns for independence for Scotland. Six Scottish Nationalist MPs were elected in 2005.

The Welsh Nationalist Party campaigns for an independent Wales. In 2008 it had three MPs in Parliament.

Northern Ireland

In Northern Ireland, the political parties are split into three separate camps. On the Unionist side are the parties that are firmly committed to Northern Ireland staying in the United Kingdom. These include the Democratic Unionist Party (DUP) with nine MPs and the Ulster Unionist Party (UUP) with one MP.

On the Republican side are parties that support a united Ireland. The Social Democratic and Labour Party (SDLP) has three MPs. Sinn Fein, which campaigns for a united Ireland has five MPs. There are two parties which are non-sectarian, which means that they do not support either the Unionist or Republican side. These are the Alliance Party and the Women's Coalition.

Fringe parties

There are also a number of smaller 'fringe' parties in the UK:

- The **Green Party** campaigns for the protection of the environment. One Green MP was elected in 2010.

- The **Welsh Nationalist Party (Plaid Cymru)** campaigns for an independent Wales and had three MPs in 2013.

- The **UK Independence Party (UKIP)** campaigns for the United Kingdom to leave the European Union. It put up 532 candidates at the 2010 general election but won no seats. However, it won 23% of the votes in the 2013 local elections and over 130 UKIP councillors were elected.

- The **Scottish Nationalist Party (SNP)** campaigns for an independent Scotland. In 2013 the SNP had six MPs. It is the party in power in the Scottish Parliament and will hold a referendum of the Scottish electorate in 2014 to decide whether Scotland should be independent.

- The **British National Party (BNP)** is a far-right fascist party which argues that Britain should be run by white British people only.

Nigel Farage is leader of the UK Independence Party.

In groups

Forming a political party

You have been given the task of forming a political party. This means that you will have to develop a number of policies that your group believes would be for the good of the country.

You will have to develop policies on the following issues:

- The economy ■ The environment ■ Transport
- Health and social welfare ■ Europe ■ Education

Give your party a name, that reflects its political ideology. Then take it in turns to present your party's policies to the rest of the class.

After you have presented your policies, discuss in your group how your party's policies were received by the rest of the class. Would you need to change them in any way so that in an election you would receive more support from class members?

Taking a vote

In groups

Here are a number of statements on some contemporary social issues. On your own, decide whether you agree or disagree with each statement, and think about whether anyone you know or anything you've seen or read has influenced your opinion on that particular issue. Then share your opinions in a group or class discussion.

1 If a young person is unemployed it is because they have not tried hard enough to find themselves a job.

2 The possession of cannabis should be decriminalised.

3 There is too much sex and violence on television.

4 The monarchy should be abolished.

5 Capital punishment should be reintroduced for the crime of murder.

6 There should be stricter controls on asylum seekers and the granting of refugee status.

How would you vote?

Look again at what the different political parties stand for (pages 74–75). Decide which political party you would vote for if there was to be a general election tomorrow. Explain the reasons for your choice.

To vote or not to vote

Although everyone over the age of 18 can vote, in the 2010 general election 35% did not vote. A person who does not vote is said to abstain. People who abstain often come from one of the following five groups: poorer people, older people, women, younger voters and the least educated.

People abstain from voting for a variety of different reasons. Some of the reasons why they do not vote are:

■ they may find themselves unable to agree with all the policies put forward by any of the parties

■ they may do so as a protest against the whole political system

■ they may not have faith in any politicians doing anything for them

■ they cannot be bothered.

People who do not vote often claim they do so because 'it won't make any difference'. But abstaining is important and it does make a difference, particularly if there is a closely fought contest and the winning candidate only wins by a few votes.

Role play

In pairs, act out a scene in which a young person tries to persuade another person, who has said that they do not intend to vote, that it is important for them to do so.

In groups

"It is everyone's duty to vote. Voting should be compulsory."

"It is everyone's right to choose not to vote. To force people to vote when they choose not to do so would be to deny them their rights."

Say which of these views you agree with and why.

Some young people have their first experience of sex without fully realising the risks that can be involved. You should fully understand the health-risks and feel completely comfortable with yourself and your body before having sex.

Many people who have sex at a young age wish afterwards that they had waited longer. The aim of this unit is to make you aware of what is meant by safer sex and to give you information about sexually transmitted infections (STIs).

What is safer sex?

There's no such thing as totally safe sex. There's always some risk of pregnancy or infection involved. 'Safer sex' means trying to cut down the risk of catching an infection, unwanted pregnancies or emotional discomfort. Although health experts can offer advice about sexual behaviour that is likely to keep you safe from these risks, nothing is 100% safe. That's why you hear people talk of 'safer sex' rather than safe sex.

In groups

1 What is meant by safer sex?

2 Why do adolescents run a greater risk of catching STIs?

"I knew my boyfriend had other partners before me, as he was five years older than me. When he wanted to have sex, I just let him because I knew otherwise I'd lose him, even though I didn't feel ready. When I suggested we should use a condom, he just laughed and said he had never bothered with things like that. It was only afterwards when I found out that he'd given me an infection that I realised my mistake." **Anna**

Four rules for safer sex

Adolescents are at risk because young people's sexual relations are often unplanned, sporadic and, sometimes, the result of coercion. Sexual relations typically occur before adolescents have gained experience and knowledge in self-protection.

Wait until you are ready. The first way of practising safer sex is not to have sex until you are absolutely sure that you are ready.

Never have unprotected sex. Whenever you have sex use a barrier method of contraception – the condom. Other methods of contraception can stop unwanted pregnancies but do not offer protection against sexually transmitted infections. Everyone can get condoms for free in Britain, from places including contraception clinics, some GP surgeries and young people centres.

Stick to fewer partners. The fewer partners you have, the less chance you have of catching an infection.

Avoid high-risk sexual activities. The most risky activity is having unprotected anal intercourse. That's because during anal intercourse the anus easily becomes damaged, and any infected body fluids can then enter the bloodstream.

3 Discuss Anna's experience. Do you think this situation is unusual? What could Anna have done differently?

Sexually transmitted infections

Sexually transmitted infections

What are STIs?

Sexually transmitted infections (STIs) are infections that are passed from one person to another during sexual contact. The infections affect the genital area, as well as the bladder, so they are known as genito-urinary infections.

Altogether there are over 20 different types of sexually transmitted infections. These include chlamydia, syphilis, genital herpes, genital warts and gonorrhoea.

How do you get infected?

An STI can only be caught through having sex with an infected partner. But STIs are very common, and anyone who has sex can get infected. It's not true that only people who have lots of partners get infected. However, the more partners you have the more you put yourself at risk.

Can sexually transmitted infections be treated?

Most STIs can be treated quickly and easily, provided they are detected at an early stage. However, some can cause long-term problems, such as infertility, if they are not treated.

There is no known cure for the HIV virus (see pages 80–81).

How can you tell if you've got an STI?

Some STIs give you symptoms that show you that there is something wrong. However, many infections, including HIV, often give no signs, so the infection can remain undetected for years. So if you have had unprotected sex it's very important to have regular checks to make sure you're not infected.

Symptoms that may indicate you have an STI are:

✗ an unusual discharge from the vagina or penis
✗ a burning sensation when you urinate or have sex
✗ spots or sores on the vagina or penis
✗ itchiness or rashes around the genital area
✗ warts on the vagina or penis.

How can I protect myself from STIs?

By being very choosy about who you have sex with, and by practising safer sex, you stand a good chance of avoiding the infections altogether. Don't allow yourself to be pressurised into having unprotected sex.

HPV is a common sexually transmitted infection. All girls aged 12 to 13 are offered HPV (human papilloma virus) vaccination as part of the NHS childhood vaccination programme. The vaccine protects against cervical cancer. The HPV vaccine is currently given as a series of three injections within a 12-month period.

What to do if you think you have an STI

There's nothing 'shameful' about catching an STI, and there's really no need to be embarrassed or worried what other people will think, so you should never be put off doing something about it.

What you need to do is find your nearest STI clinic or doctor's surgery. STI clinics are usually friendly, helpful and discreet. You don't have to give your real name or any details about yourself if you don't want to, and no one else will ever know you've been there. You don't need an appointment or a referral from your GP and the whole thing is free. All in all, a visit to an STI clinic is not the big deal you might fear, so there is no excuse for not going.

You can find out where your nearest clinic is by looking up 'sexually transmitted disease' or 'venereal disease'.

Chlamydia

Chlamydia is the most common STI in young people. Figures show that 10% of sexually active teenagers in the UK have chlamydia. The problem with chlamydia is that there are often no symptoms, so people do not know that they have the infection.

Chlamydia is caused by a bacteria and can easily be passed from one person to another, especially if they have sex without using a condom. However, if it is diagnosed early enough, it can be treated with a course of antibiotics, which will cure the infection in two weeks. Left untreated it can lead to pelvic inflammatory disease and infertility.

For your file

'Dear Lucy, I'm worried. I got drunk and had sex with someone I'd only just met. I think I may have caught a sexually transmitted infection. How can I tell? What should I do?'
Sam

Write Lucy's reply to Sam.

HIV and AIDS

The facts AIDS

What is AIDS?

AIDS stands for Acquired Immune Deficiency Syndrome. As there is no cure, AIDS is a fatal disease – though there are treatments that can prolong life. Here are the facts about AIDS.

■ AIDS is caused by a virus called HIV, which stands for Human Immunodeficiency Virus. People who are infected with HIV usually go on to develop AIDS.

■ There is no vaccine that can protect you from HIV or AIDS.

■ People carry the HIV virus in their blood and other body fluids, like semen and vaginal fluid.

■ You catch the HIV virus from other people who are infected with it.

■ *Anyone* can get infected by the HIV virus. You don't have to be gay, promiscuous or a drug-user.

■ It's impossible to tell who has got AIDS or HIV and who hasn't without a blood test. This is because people infected with HIV often don't seem ill, feel ill or look any different from anyone else until they start to develop AIDS. This can happen as much as ten years after getting infected.

■ When you have sex, you and your partner come into contact with one another's fluids. If one of you has HIV, the other could get infected.

■ The only way to help protect yourself and your partner is to use a condom when you have sex.

You can't catch the HIV virus by ...

■ touching an infected person, holding hands with them or hugging them

■ using things an infected person has used (like phones, headphones, books, soap or towels)

■ sitting where an infected person has sat (including on toilets) or wearing clothes they have worn

■ using the same shower or swimming pool or sharing things like food, knives and forks, plates, cups and make-up

■ an infected person breathing, sneezing or coughing near you.

How you can catch HIV

You catch the HIV virus when an infected person's body fluids enter your body, and there are ways this can happen that don't involve sex. The good news is that these risks are quite easily avoided:

■ If an infected person was bleeding and you also happened to have an open wound – even a scratch or a small cut – there would be a chance that some of their blood could enter your bloodstream if you touched them.

  If you have to clean up someone else's blood, always wear rubber gloves to protect yourself.

■ If you're a drug-user who injects drugs and you share a needle with an infected person, you would run a very high risk of getting infected. The only way a drug-user can stay safe is always to use a fresh needle and syringe.

  If you ever find a syringe or needle lying around, don't touch it – it could be infected.

■ Anything that has had blood on it is a potential hazard. If you are considering having a tattoo, acupuncture or electrolysis, or getting your ears pierced, you should always check that the equipment has been properly sterilised before it is used on you.

  It's not a good idea to share a toothbrush or wet-shave razor with anyone, because of the risk of blood from bleeding gums or shaving cuts.

How can you tell if you are infected with HIV?

There are no immediate symptoms, so the only way to tell is by having a blood test. This is not really an AIDS test, because it tests for antibodies to HIV, and it may be a long time before someone who is HIV-positive develops the symptoms of AIDS, if at all. HIV tests can be carried out free and in confidence at your local genito-urinary clinic.

In groups

1 Discuss what you have learned from the article 'AIDS – the facts' on page 80. What is the HIV virus? How can it be transmitted? Who is at risk? What precautions should you take to avoid becoming infected?

2 Draw up a test-yourself quiz consisting of statements about AIDS, some of which are true and some of which are false. Then give your quiz to another group to do.

For your file

Design a page for a website that gives teenagers essential information about AIDS.

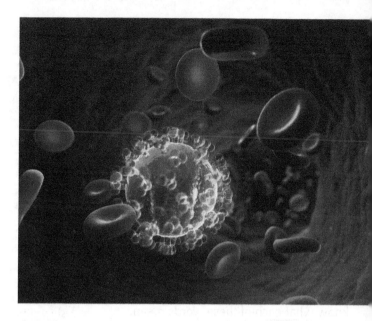

Attitudes to sex

Young people have widely differing views about sex and AIDS, as these comments show.

"I think sex before marriage is wrong. If people wait until they are married and stick to one partner, then the AIDS problem would be solved. It only exists because people don't behave responsibly and sleep around."

"I don't see anything wrong with experimenting while you're young and having lots of partners. AIDS doesn't bother me. Why should it?"

"Of course I'm concerned about AIDS, but I'm not going to let it stand in the way of my having sex. But that doesn't mean I intend to jump into bed with someone at the first opportunity. I think it's important to develop a relationship first."

"People need to learn to be sensible and responsible about sex. Too many people I know take unnecessary risks. If you're going to have sex with someone you need to care for them and that involves thinking about all the possible consequences of having sex."

"Adults keep on and on about the risks of having sex, but I think they're exaggerating. It's just a matter of luck whether you catch an infection or get yourself pregnant."

Teenagers think HIV is 'irrelevant'

Teenagers think that HIV is 'nothing to do with them', according to a health education survey published to mark World AIDS Day.

The study of 16–18-year-olds found that the majority saw the virus as 'irrelevant to people their age'. Most knew about its effects and how it was transmitted but were still unlikely to use a condom.

The teenagers saw AIDS as an issue for 'promiscuous older people' and saw condoms as an 'inconvenience'.

In 2011 there were 96,000 people living with HIV in the UK. Around a quarter of these people were unaware of their HIV infection.

In groups

1 Read the quotes in the section 'Attitudes to sex', then discuss the views. What is your attitude towards sex, relationships and marriage?

2 What is your attitude towards AIDS? Do you see it as 'irrelevant', as the teenagers in the survey did?

Share your views with those of other groups in a class discussion.

Understanding prices

A price is the amount of money that you pay for something. In the UK, most prices are fixed. In other words, what you see advertised is the price that you will pay.

Different shops will sell different things at different prices. This is because it's up to each individual seller (or 'retailer', if they have a shop) to decide what they think the goods are worth.

In order to sell more goods, sellers use a whole range of words and promotions to make us buy. It's therefore important to know what each of these words mean.

In groups

1 'It's a bargain!' Share your experiences of buying something you think was a bargain, because you shopped around to get it for a good price.

2 'It's a rip-off!' Talk about times when you think you've been ripped off, because you bought something at what you considered a fair price, only to find out later that it was being offered elsewhere at a much cheaper price.

For your file

Visit one of the following websites where you can barter and swap something. Which site do you think is best? Why? Write a short report on which site you would use and what you would swap and why.

www.swapz.co.uk
www.swapitshop.com
www.swapcycle.co.uk

Is the price right?

Your questions about prices

Do all shop goods have to have prices marked on them?

● No. The law states that: Shops and supermarkets have to show the price of food and drink.
● Garages must show the price of petrol per litre.
● Pubs, cafés and restaurants must have a list showing the prices of various drinks and food they serve. Most food prices are shown in a menu.
● Cafés and restaurants also have to indicate whether tips are included or not.

Does a shop have to serve me something at the marked price? Even if they have made a mistake?

No. Shops are not legally required to sell a customer anything. Of course, most will want to help you, and some good retailers will honour a mistake.

What happens if I order some goods in advance, and then I'm told later the price has gone up?

If you agreed the price in advance, and can prove this in writing (e.g. with a delivery order) the shop will have to honour the original price.

How do I tell if price reductions are genuine?

Shop around. Many shops will sell goods at a higher price for 28 days. Then they can legally reduce the price, and claim it is a price reduction. Always compare with other shops, and on the internet.

BOGOF – buy one, get one free. e.g. you could buy two cans of cola for the price of one.

Discount – a lower price to encourage you to buy. Discounts are usually set as a percentage (e.g. 10% off).

RRP – the recommended retail price. This is how much the person who made the goods – the manufacturer – thinks it ought to be sold for.

Special price – this is a sales trick. A special price is simply a way for a retailer to encourage you to buy.

Unit price – this tells you how much you pay for a particular quantity of goods. For example, the unit price of one bar of chocolate lets you know how good a deal it is if you buy a whole box of chocolate bars.

VAT – value added tax. This is a tax that is levied on most goods, but not food, drink, books or children's clothes.

Other systems of buying and selling

In some countries, prices aren't fixed and different systems of buying and selling are used.

Haggling

My name is Khaing. I live in Myanmar. I work at a local market here in Myanmar where we don't have fixed prices. Instead, when we want to buy something, the seller suggests his price. You then have to make an offer. This is what you are willing to pay. We then argue about the price until we agree. This is called haggling.

Sometimes this can take a long time. Also, you have to be careful you don't agree too high a price. Usually, it's best to start at 25% of what the seller is asking, and agree at about 50% of what they want.

Bartering

My name is Lu. I live in rural China. Often, we barter goods here. This is when you exchange one good directly for another. There's no money involved. It's just like swapping things. It's good, because we are able to trade things directly. However, sometimes you have to wait until you have the right thing available to swap for what you want.

What do people think?

"I often barter small things with friends. It's a great way to recycle things without throwing them out"
– Sasha, Birmingham

"I hate haggling – I much prefer to know what something is going to cost"
– Christine, Standlake

"I love haggling – it works for those who are good at it. I saved a lot when I bought my last car just by holding out."
– Simon, Newcastle

"Bartering is great now that there's the internet, because you can find things to swap with other people online."
– Lucas, Cornwall

Did you know?

It's possible to haggle at some places in the UK. Markets, car boot sales, house clearances, buying a car – all can involve some haggling. However, you won't usually be able to haggle on the High Street: people will just think you are being rude.

In groups

Read the two case studies, and how people feel about them. What are the advantages and disadvantages of haggling and bartering compared to having fixed prices? Give reasons for your views.

Consumer rights

If you buy something from a retailer, there are certain laws which govern the sale. These help protect your rights as a consumer.

Know your consumer rights

What can you expect?

When somebody sells you something, there are several conditions that should be met:

- the goods should be of satisfactory quality. If you bought a pair of shoes, they shouldn't have a hole in them
- the goods should be fit for purpose. It's no good buying a DVD player if it only plays Japanese DVDs, when you live in the UK
- the goods should be as described. If you order a black leather jacket, you can refuse and demand your money back if a brown jacket turns up.

What can you get back?

There may be a problem with something when you buy it. If so, you can ask for one of the following by law:

- all of your money back
- some of the money back if the goods are slightly damaged
- for the goods to be replaced or repaired.

Some traders, particularly big companies, make extra promises. Often they say they will issue a refund or an exchange for unused goods within a short time period, such as 21or 28

days. This creates useful extra consumer rights.

When don't you get your money back?

However, there are some situations where you won't get your money back. These include:

- if you were told of a problem before you bought the product
- if there was an obvious fault that you should have noticed before buying (e.g. a second hand bicycle had some broken spokes)
- if you made a mistake (e.g. you ordered a black leather jacket, but decided you wanted a brown one)

- if you have seen the product cheaper elsewhere or have just changed your mind
- if you caused any damage to the product (e.g. you bought some sunglasses but you broke them).

Who can help me if I've got a problem?

A Citizen's Advice Bureau or CAB can help with consumer rights. This can give free, neutral legal advice on a wide range of areas. CABs can be found in most major towns in the UK. The address will be in your local telephone directory.

For your file

Use the information on this page to draw up a list of 10 facts you need to know about your rights as a consumer.

Role play

In pairs, role play a scene in which one of you demands a refund from a shopkeeper for an item that they sold you, but which broke the first time you used it.

In pairs

Study the information on this page. Then draw up a quiz consisting of statements about consumer rights, some of which are true and some of which are false. Give your quiz to another pair to do. Which of you knows more about consumer right

Buying the right mobile phone

There are lots of things to think about when buying a mobile phone.

Pay as you go phones

This is when you buy the phone and then pay for what you use. So if you want 100 minutes of call time, you pay for it in advance. When you run out of minutes, you buy more with a top-up card.

Advantages

- You are not locked into any contract. You only pay for what you use.
- If you don't like your phone provider, or see a better deal, you can change anytime.

Disadvantages

- They can work out more expensive than contract phones if you use them a lot.
- You have to buy the handset
- You can run out of minutes

Contract phones

This means you sign a contract with a mobile phone company. You agree to pay them for a certain number of minutes and texts each month, costing a set amount. The handset would usually be free with a contract phone. This amount does not change over the contract. This is when you buy the phone and then pay for what you use. Contracts usually last for 12, 18 or 24 months.

Advantages

- Contracts usually last for 12, 18 or 24 months.
- You can get lots of free minutes and if you use your phone lots, it is good value for money.

Disadvantages

- If you are on an expensive contract and prices fall you can lose out
- If you never use all the minutes or texts allowed, you're paying for a service that you are not using.

Watch out!

Don't get locked into a contract that is too expensive.

Make sure you aren't paying for minutes and texts you don't use.

Make sure that you aren't having to top-up your contract with extra minutes and texts.

Make sure you don't sign up to lots of extra services that you don't want, like new ringtones and text alerts. Otherwise, you'll be hit with a BIG BILL.

Whatever type of phone you choose, you need to read the small print very carefully. Make sure there are no hidden surprises, such as calls during the day with a 20p connection fee that is not included. If this is the case and you make a lot of daytime calls, you're going to be wasting money.

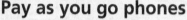

Role play

In pairs, role play a scene in which two friends discuss how to get the best deal and what things they need to consider when buying a mobile phone.

In groups

Make a list of all the different things you have to consider when buying a mobile phone. Do this on your own or in pairs. Rank each item in order of importance. Then compare it with the lists of other people in your group. Give reasons for your views.

For your file

Write an article for a teenage magazine entitled 'Top tips – How to get the best deal out of your mobile phone'.

Being a green consumer

To help tackle climate change, we need to change our behaviour as consumers. Being green as a consumer involves doing several different things:

- using energy and materials from green sources
- recycling waste whenever possible
- reducing the amount of energy and materials we use.

This last point includes reducing our carbon footprint. Our carbon footprint is the amount of CO_2 we produce each year. This causes global warming. It is measured by each tonne of the gas we produce. Most of our CO_2 comes from the way we travel – particularly air travel from long flights. Car pollution is another major source of CO_2.

We need to be more green at home, when we are shopping and when we are travelling.

Going green at home

Going green starts at home. Some obvious things we can do to be more green in the house include:

- switching off lights when they aren't being used
- installing energy-efficient light bulbs
- composting to reduce the amount of rubbish we throw out
- washing clothes at a lower temperature (e.g. 30°C not 40°C)
- recycling whenever possible.

Wind turbine – to produce electricity

Solar panels – to produce electricity

Three-storey house – to preserve heat

Mid-terrace house – to preserve heat

Compost bin – to collect green waste for composting

Water butts – to collect water for gardening

A 'green' house

One form of green energy is micro-generation. This is when a house produces some of its own electricity. In the UK, this is usually solar panels.

For your file

There are many internet sites which help you to calculate your carbon footprint. Look up what yours is, then write about what you could do to reduce it.

Visit the Eden Project website www.edenproject.com and write a paragraph about it.

Disposable plastic objects can harm and even kill marine life

Green shopping

Green shopping is about reducing the amount of energy and materials we consume. This can be done in a variety of ways.

Packaging. Each year, the UK produces about 10 million tonnes of packaging waste, which is 24% of all household waste. In 2009, a survey of food packaging showed that almost 40% of supermarket packaging could not be recycled. Retailers are being urged to do more to reduce the amount of packaging for their goods. A good way to avoid packaging-waste, would be to choose loose fruit and vegetables where you can.

Plastic bags. Shops in the UK gave out 9.9 billion plastic bags in 2008. These fill up landfill sites, can kill marine life and form a significant part of litter. The Irish government has put a tax on plastic bags, which has cut their use dramatically, and some countries, such as Bangladesh, have banned plastic bags altogether. When you go shopping, try to take a 'bag for life' with you, or a rucksack to carry your shopping home.

Becoming vegetarian. Using land for producing meat is a lot less productive than for using it to grow vegetables. Four hectares of land (about five football pitches) will support:

- 2 people eating cattle meat
- 10 people eating maize
- 24 people eating wheat
- 61 people eating soya beans.

In addition, there is the energy and gas produced from raising cattle, which needs to be considered.

Buying organic and locally-grown food. Organic food is produced with no chemicals. This means that no pesticides that damage the environment are used. However, there is little point buying organic food that has been flown half-way around the world. This is because of the energy used to get it here. Instead, there is now a movement amongst green consumers to support local farmers. Food is now measured in food miles – how many miles the food has travelled to get to the supermarket. The greenest food is organic *and* local.

Buying ozone-friendly products. Ozone is a a gas high up in the air that protects us from being burnt by the sun. Certain chemicals, called CFCs (chlorofluorocarbon), damage this ozone layer. These chemicals are usually found in aerosols like deodorants. Ozone-friendly products do not have any CFCs. They are a green alternative.

Being a green tourist

We took a green holiday this year. Rather than going away to Europe or America, we went to Cornwall. So we didn't fly – which is really important. Taking just one long-haul flight can produce the same amount of CO_2 as driving a car for a year!

We didn't even drive to Cornwall. Instead we used our family railcard and took the train. So we avoided all the traffic jams and we didn't miss driving around, because we took our bikes with us on the train.

The hotel was very green. It had solar panels to provide heating and lighting had energy-efficient light bulbs. The lights on the stairs and in the corridors were on time switches, so they were only on when necessary. We had to ask for our towels to be washed. Many hotels I know waste a lot of water by changing the towels each day even if it's not necessary.

Sam, London

In pairs

Pick one area – going green at home, green shopping or being a green tourist. Discuss which of these things you already do. Which changes do you think would be easiest to make? Compare your answers and give reasons for your views.

Globalisation

In the 21st century it is important to see yourself not only as a UK citizen, but as a citizen of Europe and of the world. This unit examines some key global issues and how they affect everybody.

One of the most important developments in recent years has been the spread of globalisation. Globalisation is the term used to describe the process whereby people, governments and businesses throughout the world are becoming increasingly dependent on one another.

Multinationals

One of the main causes of globalisation has been the development of huge multinational corporations whose businesses operate in many different countries.

Another cause of globalisation has been the technological revolution that began in the latter half of the 20th century. Developments in transport mean that people and goods can be moved swiftly from one part of the world to another. Developments in communication mean that information can be sent across the world in seconds via the internet, e-mail, fax and telephone.

Multinational corporations

Multinationals (sometimes called transnationals) are major business corporations that have subsidiaries, investments or operations in more than one country. According to the United Nations, multinationals are associations that 'possess and control means of production or services outside the country in which they were established'. Some multinationals are viewed as threats to national sovereignty, exerting undue influence to achieve their corporate goals or sacrificing human and environmental well-being in order to maximise profits. Annual sales of some multinationals exceed $100 billion, far greater than the exports and imports of most less economically developed countries.

Multinationals include:

- Media corporations, for example News International
- Computer companies, for example Microsoft
- Oil companies, for example Royal Dutch/Shell, Exxon
- Motor companies, for example Ford, Toyota
- Supermarket corporations, for example Wal-Mart Stores Inc.

Globalisation – what do you think?

"Globalisation is a good thing, because the more people come to see themselves as citizens of the world, the less conflicts there are likely to be."

"It gives too much power to multinational corporations whose decisions can influence world trade as much as the decisions of governments, but they are not accountable to anybody except their shareholders."

"In one sense, it's a good idea for countries to be inter-dependent. In another, it's dangerous. A crisis in one country could easily lead to problems in others. Globalisation has its disadvantages as well as its advantages."

In groups, discuss what you understand by the term 'globalisation'. What are the main causes of globalisation? What do you think the effects of globalisation will be? Do you view it as a good thing or a bad thing? Explain why.

Supermarkets and sweatshops

Supermarkets today wield unprecedented power on a global scale. From Bangladesh to Bristol, supermarkets dictate the terms in which producers are forced to sell their goods. Supermarkets seek to keep prices low and their own profits high. With threats to find new suppliers, they force prices down around the world.

However, the workers who produce those goods – from fruit and vegetables to flowers and cheap clothes – feel their impact every day. Working in factories or on plantations, they face long hours, terrible working conditions and little or no trade union rights. Despite working 80 hours a week, many workers are unable to earn a living wage (a wage which is high enough to maintain a normal standard of living).

For example, in Bangalore, India, garment workers have to work 9–10 hours a day. They are forced to complete very high hourly targets. Many get paid well under a living wage, yet they are expected to take care of a family. Overtime is not paid, workplace harassment and abuse are rampant, but they cannot voice their opinions through unions.

The real price of trainers
Made in Indonesia – sold in the UK

Factory 12%
(wages 0.4%
materials 8%
other 1.6%
profit 2%)

Transport & tax 5%

Shoe company 33%
(research 11%
publicity 8.5%
profit 13.5%)

Retail store 50%

A pair of trainers can cost more to buy in the UK than the worker who made them receives in a month.

Stamping out sweatshops

Campaigners against sweatshops, such as No Sweat, demand an end to sweatshop labour, including forced overtime and excessive hours.

They campaign for workers in sweatshops to be free to organise their own independent trade union.

They suggest that there should be a labour mark on garments sold in the UK, so that we can have a guarantee that they were produced by workers who were free to organise and set decent standards in their workplace.

In groups

What can people in the UK do to bring an end to sweatshop labour? What do you think of the idea of introducing a labour mark on garments? Would it stop you buying goods that are produced by sweatshop labour?

For your file

'We should boycott goods that are produced in sweatshops, even though it may mean paying more for the things we want.' Write a statement saying why you agree or disagree with this view.

The internet

One of the major driving forces behind globalisation has been the development of the internet. The internet enables information to be exchanged with speed and ease across the world.

The communications revolution brought about by the internet has affected people's lives worldwide. In 2012, there were 3.3 billion e-mail accounts worldwide. This is estimated to rise to 4.3 billion by 2016.

The internet – positive and negative effects

✓ Information can be sent in seconds rather than days or weeks.

✗ It has reduced personal contact and face-to-face meetings.

✓ It is possible to do business by e-mail across continents without any barriers.

✗ The internet can be used for criminal as well as legal activities.

✓ You can research any topic much more quickly than when you had to rely on libraries and books.

✗ Not all data on the internet is accurate. It can be difficult to separate what is biased and inaccurate information from what is reliable and accurate.

✓ You can communicate with your family and friends wherever they are and chat to people from other parts of the world on social networking sites.

✗ Your privacy may be compromised. Many users do not realise that what they put online about themselves will stay there forever.

✓ The internet has changed the way people shop. You can compare prices and buy goods online without having to travel to different stores.

✗ Not all shopping sites are reliable. You may find you have paid for goods that do not arrive or that are faulty or not as described. Also, many people believe this type of shopping has had a detrimental effect on the British high street.

In groups

Discuss the effects of the internet. Do the positive effects outweigh the negative effects?

For your file

'The arrival of the internet has done more harm than good.' Explain why you agree or disagree with this view.

Problems of the internet

The development of the internet has produced problems as well as benefits. There has been a great increase in what has become known as e-crime. This ranges from fraud and identity theft to cyber-bullying, and from international terrorism to online paedophile grooming.

Dealing with e-crime is one of the major challenges facing governments around the world.

Policing the internet

Measures that have been suggested to protect young people from viewing harmful material include:

- a website rating system, similar to that used for films

- industry-wide take-down times, requiring sites such as Facebook or YouTube to remove offensive material in a specified timeframe

- changing libel laws to enable people to take legal action if they are defamed online.

Cybercrime

"The global nature of the internet has allowed criminals to commit almost any illegal activity anywhere in the world, making it essential for all countries to adapt their domestic offline controls to cover crimes carried out in cyberspace. The use of the internet by terrorists, particularly for recruitment and the incitement of radicalisation, poses a serious threat to national and international security." **Interpol**

"The internet is useful, but the negative effects it has on society far outweigh its usefulness. It allows criminals and terrorists the ability to carry out their activities more easily and more efficiently." **Tamar**

Lara's story

Lara Coton knows about the dangers of putting photos on the net. The teenager from Tamworth sent an innocent photo from a family beach holiday to an art website, and was horrified to find it had been used as the cover of an X-rated movie.

In groups

Freedom of speech is a good idea, but some censorship is necessary. For example, Jihadist sites which encourage terrorism should be closed down.' Discuss this view.

Discuss the ideas for policing the internet. What others can you suggest?

Global warming

Global warming is the term used to describe the increase in the average world temperatures brought about by human activities. It is seen by many scientists as the most serious threat to the world's environment.

The greenhouse effect

Global warming is caused by what is known as the 'greenhouse effect'. This is the name given to the process in which certain gases in the lower atmosphere allow the sun's rays through to heat the surface of the Earth, then trap a proportion of the heat as it is radiated back into space. It is called the greenhouse effect because the gases in the atmosphere are acting like the panes of glass in a greenhouse to trap the heat.

Without the greenhouse effect the Earth would be unable to support life, because the temperature on the surface would be too low. During the last 100 years, however, human activities have altered the levels of some of the greenhouse gases in the atmosphere. This has caused global warming.

In groups

Discuss what you learn from this page about global warming. What is the greenhouse effect? What human activities have increased the greenhouse effect? What are the effects of global warming?

Greenhouse gases

Carbon dioxide (CO_2) is one of the main greenhouse gases. The level of CO_2 in the atmosphere has increased by nearly 30% since pre-industrial times.

One reason for the increase is deforestation. Forests affect the amount of CO_2 in the atmosphere because trees take in CO_2 from the air as they grow. When forests are cleared and burned, there are fewer trees to take in the CO_2. As the world's forests are destroyed to provide land for the landless poor or for commercial logging, nearly 2 billion tonnes of CO_2 are released into the atmosphere each year through forest burning.

But the main source of CO_2 from human activity is through the burning of fossil fuels to provide energy in power stations, factories and motor vehicles. The countries mainly responsible for the production of CO_2 are the industrialised countries of the developed world.

Other gases that contribute to the greenhouse effect are:

- **methane**, which is released into the atmosphere by agricultural activities, waste disposal and during coal-mining and oil exploration

- **nitrous oxide**, which is a by-product of industrial and agricultural processes, such as the use of nitrogenous fertilisers.

The effects of global warming

Research by the Intergovernmental Panel on Climate Change suggests that at the present rate of carbon emissions global average temperatures will rise 2°C by 2050.

It also reported that the ten warmest years on record had occurred between 1997 and 2008.

Storms – storms and hurricanes will become more frequent and stronger as oceans heat up, causing more water to evaporate.

Droughts – continental heartlands will dry out more in summer.

Floods – there will be increased flooding in coastal areas and river estuaries such as Bangladesh and the Nile Delta; London and many other British coastal cities will also be threatened.

Geo-engineering

Geo-engineering involves developing a technical solution that will cool the planet if global warming continues to accelerate.

Ideas being researched include

- placing millions of tiny mirrors in space to reflect back some of the sun's rays
- using rockets to launch tonnes of sulphur into the stratosphere to form a kind of planetary sunshade
- spraying sea water into the atmosphere to make it cloudier
- burying CO_2 produced by burning fossil fuels under the sea in exhausted oil and gas reservoirs.

However, there are many unanswered questions about geo-engineering. Would it work? Could it be reversed if it didn't work? What might any side effects be?

An energy policy for the 21st century

In developing an energy policy for the 21st century we need to look at ways of meeting our energy needs that are economic, efficient and will not damage the environment.

We need to promote energy conservation, by improving the efficiency of current methods of energy production and lessening the environmental damage they cause.

At the same time, we need to develop renewable energy resources, such as wind power, water power and solar power, so that we depend less and less on energy from fossil fuels.

In groups

1 Discuss what governments can do to reduce CO_2 emissions and cut down global warming. Why is it difficult to get international agreement on this issue?

2 Discuss the ideas for geo-engineering. Do you think they are far-fetched or might they be the answer to global warming?

3 Discuss what businesses and institutions such as schools can do to use energy more efficiently. Carry out a survey to find out how efficiently energy is being used in your school buildings. Look at such factors as insulation, the energy efficiency of electrical goods, whether lights and appliances are left running unnecessarily and building design. Draft a report, based on your findings, making suggestions as to how the school could save energy.

4 Discuss what individuals can do to change their energy habits and reduce their energy use, for example, alter how they use transport, support recycling schemes. Talk about how these actions would save energy. What other ways of conserving energy can you suggest?

For your file

Write a letter to a newspaper saying why you are concerned about global warming and what you think needs to be done about it.

Slow the global warming

It is important to slow the warming as much as possible. This means using less fossil fuel, and slowing down deforestation. This can be best achieved through:

- **energy conservation**, including better use of public transport and cleaner, more efficient cars
- **energy efficiency**, by greater use of gas which produces less CO_2 than coal and oil, and through renewable energy such as solar power
- **stopping the destruction of rain forests** (deforestation) and starting to replace trees (afforestation) to soak up carbon dioxide.

Keeping the peace

The United Nations (UN) was set up in October 1945 after the end of the Second World War. It is an association of countries that aims to promote international peace, security and co-operation.

The UN Security Council

The Security Council is the UN body responsible for debating and taking decisions on conflict situations. It has five permanent members: China, France, Russia, the UK and the USA. The other ten members are elected for 2 years. The five permanent members have the power to veto any decisions they don't agree with.

Because the UN Security Council could not agree to take military action against Iraq in 2003, the US-led coalition, which included Britain, decided to take action without waiting for UN approval.

Why has the UN failed to bring peace?

The power of the veto in the Security Council means that when conflicts occur the UN cannot agree on what action to take.

Even when there is agreement to send peacekeeping troops into conflict areas, the UN has stopped short of giving them the authority to take the decisive action necessary to be effective.

For example, in the Democratic Republic of Congo, despite the presence of UN peacekeepers, fighting has continued between government troops and rebels. One million people were made homeless there during 2007 and 2008. Similarly, sending a UN peacekeeping force to the Dafur region of Sudan has failed to bring peace.

Critics argue that the UN will continue to be ineffective until it is prepared to commit its troops to take firmer military action, even if this means UN troops getting more involved in conflicts than they have done in the past.

A shattered dream

The UN's founding charter proclaimed its mission to save 'succeeding generations from the scourge of war'. It would tackle global poverty to bring about higher standards of living everywhere. The UN system was supposed to 'harmonise the actions of nations', preventing the clashes that had led to two world wars. After 60 difficult years, and despite some significant achievements, it faces a grim reality. Local wars are widespread. Although living standards have improved in parts of the world, tens of millions still starve or die young. Most damagingly, the vision of an international body that could sort out arguments between nations has not been realised.

 In groups

Discuss what you have learned from the information on this page about how the UN has attempted to bring peace to the world and why so far it has failed.

Arms exports

CAMPAIGN AGAINST ARMS TRADE

Fuel wars

Millions of people have been killed in wars since 1945. Most of these wars, which make the world a more dangerous place for us all, have been fought with imported arms.

Waste resources

The purchase and production of arms wastes resources, diverting finance, skills and materials that could be used to ensure that everyone has food, clean water, housing, health care and education.

Support repressive regimes

British arms are often sold to governments, like that of Indonesia, which have appalling human rights records. Such sales legitimise these regimes and further demoralise their peoples.

The arms trade

Many of the wars that have taken place since 1945 have been in the developing world. The arms that have been used in them have mostly come from the developed world.

Over three-quarters of the arms traded are manufactured by the five permanent members of the UN Security Council. The USA has sold weapons or training to almost 90% of the countries it has identified as harbouring terrorists.

It is often difficult to establish where the arms used in conflicts have originated. However, according to the Campaign Against the Arms Trade, cases of the use of UK arms in conflict zones include:

- by Libya against 'rebels' in 2011
- by Israel in the attack on Gaza in 2009
- by US troops in the invasion of Iraq
- by Argentina in the Falklands war.

The UK and the arms trade

In 2013, the British government approved £12 billion of arms exports to countries with poor human rights records, such as Israel, Saudi Arabia, China and Zimbabwe.

> "It is difficult to imagine any other British industry which could cause death and injury on a large scale and remain not merely unaccountable but receive large sums of taxpayers' money in export credit guarantees."
> Oxfam report, *Small Arms, Wrong Hands*

> "Aid donors like Britain are quick to chide the poor for spending too much on arms – yet they are slow to apply the same standards to our own military budgets or to the way we train and sell arms to those very same countries."
> World Development Movement leaflet

In groups

> "It's all very well to suggest that the UK shouldn't manufacture and sell arms, but why should we stop doing so and sacrifice British jobs? Unless all countries agree to do so – and there's no hope of that – we'd only be punishing ourselves."

> "Someone somewhere has got to do something that will stop the senseless slaughter. Britain should show the way and stop exporting arms to anyone anywhere."

Discuss these views of the arms trade.

For your file

Write your views on the arms trade and the part the UK plays in it.

Pressure groups

If we want to show that we think those who govern us have done something wrong or are about to make a wrong decision, we have to protest in some way. Individually what we can do is take the matter up with our MP or the local council. However, if it's an important issue, there may be a pressure group that we can join.

A pressure group is a group of people who try to influence the local or national government to change their policy by mounting a publicity campaign to get their point across. The aim of a campaign is to bring facts about the issue to the attention of as many people as possible, putting forward the reasons why the people in power should make a different decision. If enough protesters make their objections clear, the decision could be altered.

BULLS DIE A BLOODY DEATH IN PAMPLONA

Pressure group techniques

Pressure groups use a variety of techniques to achieve their aims. These are generally lawful, but some groups choose to break the law to promote their cause.

Lawful pressure

Pressure groups sometimes contact politicians by sending a deputation to meet MPs and to put their case. They often try to gain coverage in the media, to argue their point of view. This can be done in many ways, for example by adverts, press releases and media stunts.

A favoured method by pressure groups is dedicating a particular day or week to a specific cause.

Unlawful pressure

Sometimes pressure groups use civil disobedience to promote their cause. This is when a person chooses to break the law in a non-violent way, for example, by sitting down in the path of a mechanical digger to prevent it from entering a construction site.

A few pressure groups break the law by violent protest. One example is the Animal Liberation Front, which has attacked and fire-bombed laboratories involved in animal experiments.

In groups

What issues do you feel so strongly about that you would be prepared to campaign for them?

Think about:

changes to the appearance of the area where you live – knocking down an attractive part of town or building a motorway through peaceful countryside

changes to the facilities of your area – closing down a swimming pool or youth centre, building on a football pitch

changes to the safety of your area – a refusal by the council to improve street-lighting near an alleyway, or to put a 30mph speed restriction on the main road through a village

things you think are wrong – hunting, trials of GM crops.

Each group should decide on an issue that you would be prepared to campaign about. Then share your views in a class discussion.

In groups

Discuss the different techniques that pressure groups use. What is your view of non-violent civil disobedience? Can it be justified or should pressure groups always work within the law?

Living Streets

In 2011 there were 26,198 pedestrians injured on Britain's roads. 453 of them died. The pressure group Living Streets campaigns to make walking safer, more convenient and easier.

 In groups

 **In groups**

Discuss the hazards that pedestrians can encounter and the advice on what you should do if you encounter such hazards. What particular hazards are there for pedestrians in the area where you live?

It's time to put your foot down

Every day as a pedestrian you are likely to encounter certain hazards. Living Streets suggests what action you should take.

Building site obstructions

These hazards take many forms: scaffolding, skips and mounds of building materials. They must be licensed and lit. Check with your local council that they are.

Holes in the pavement

Holes are made by utility companies (gas, electricity, water, telephone or cable). It is required that such holes should be fenced and lit, and when the work is finished, the pavement should be restored to its previous standard. Complaints should be addressed to the utility concerned or to the council.

The same applies to access covers, which may be broken or sticking up.

Dog dirt

Local bylaws sometimes make fouling of the footway by dogs an offence. If you have such bylaws and dog owners ignore them, press your local council for enforcement.

Damaged pavements

The local authority maintains most highways. If you trip and fall over a pavement slab that's sticking up an inch (2.5 cm) or more you may have a good case for compensation.

Pavement parking

There is still no national ban on pavement parking, but you can complain to the police, especially if vehicles parked on the pavement are causing an obstruction.

Pavement cycling

This is becoming such a common practice that many people don't seem to realise it's illegal. But it is an offence. Ask your local police to step up enforcement with their powers of an on the spot fine.

No pavement?

This doesn't let the council off the hook. If there isn't a pavement, ask for one. Highway authorities have a duty to provide one where they consider it's necessary and desirable.

Pedestrian crossings

If there is no crossing where you think there should be one, or if the 'green man' time is too short to allow you to cross in safety, tell your local council.

Too fast?

Where conditions are unsafe for pedestrians because of traffic speeds, remind your local council it has powers to regulate traffic on non-trunk roads and urge the police to improve enforcement of existing regulations.

Organising a campaign to make your area safer

What campaign?

Discuss what problems there are with traffic in your area. Identify what you consider to be the main problem, and suggest what could be done about it.

Form yourselves into an action group and work together to plan a campaign to publicise the problem and to put pressure on the appropriate authorities to do something about it.

Give your action group a name

This must be a catchy name or a set of initials. For example, if you live in South Mimms, you could be 'SMASH' – 'South Mimms Action on Safety Hazards'. Or if you come from Haslemere, you could be 'HARM' – 'Haslemere Action on Road Menace'. Or you could simply call yourself after your class – the '9N Traffic Action Group', for example.

Surveying opinions and collecting information

You've decided there's a problem and what you think should be done about it, but does anyone else agree?

Find out who in the neighbourhood agrees with you by contacting the local community centre and sending someone to talk to any neighbourhood groups, for example, your local residents' or tenants' group or neighbourhood association.

Circulate a leaflet or a short questionnaire to ask local people how they feel about the issue. Ask them to express their views on what needs to be done to see if they have any alternative suggestions. Remember to get the views of some local businesses and shopkeepers as well as those of local residents.

Planning your campaign

Hold a planning meeting to discuss what you have learned from your survey of opinions about support for your campaign. Study the list (below) of things you could do as part of your campaign and decide which ones you are going to do:

● Produce posters to put up locally ● Design a website and distribute a newsletter ● Organise a petition ● Produce a press release ● Organise a media event ● Send a deputation to the local council ● Write to the local MP.

Design a website and print a newsletter

Use your IT skills to design a website and produce a newsletter explaining what the purpose of the action group is and saying what your plans are.

Follow these guidelines to help to get your message across:

● design a heading that includes the group's name and the school's address

● keep it short (two sides of A4 maximum) and break up the text with bold, eye-catching headlines

● don't assume that everyone will be aware of the problem (or that they will see it your way)

● include drawings, cartoons, diagrams or photos

● make sure there is a contact name and address.

Contacting the council

Send a copy of your newsletter and details of your website to your local councillor along with a letter inviting them to come to the school to discuss the issue with you and the rest of your class.

Hitting the headlines

To win your campaign you must get the public on your side. And there's no better way of reaching people than through the media. A story in the papers or on the radio will be read or heard by thousands of people.

Here's how to use your local media to get results:

- **Give your story an 'angle'.** Local papers are keen to write about something that is affecting local people.

- **Invite the local press** to attend any presentation you make by emailing a press release to the news editor. Email your press release to the picture desk too. But have someone ready to take your own photos too – in case the professionals are too busy to be able to come.

- **Organise an event** – anything that would make an interesting photo or radio story. You could cycle in gas masks to draw attention to air pollution or dress up as green men to publicise the need for a new pedestrian crossing.

- **Involve your MP.** Present your survey results or petition to your local MP in person – send local newspapers a press release and invite them to photograph the occasion. If your MP supports your views, they may be happy to pose with you.

How to write a good press release

Keep it short (just one side of A4 paper) and to the point.

Put the information about the date, time and place in bold type.

Get the most important information into the first couple of attention-grabbing sentences – who, what, where, when and why.

Include a quote that sums up your campaign's message. The paper can print it to save themselves the trouble of interviewing you.

If there's a lot of detail to include, put it in notes at the end.

Give a contact name and phone number at the bottom in case the journalist wants to follow up the story.

PRESS RELEASE

Photocall: Saturday 11th March 2009 11.30am Newtown Town Hall

On Saturday 11th March the N.Y.A.T.F. (Newtown Youth Against Traffic Fumes) group from Sir Albert Graham School will present their petition **STOP POLLUTING OUR STREETS** to local MP Janice Buttersworth at the Town Hall.

The petition is in protest at the problem of traffic fumes and gives suggestions of what needs to be done to clean up air quality.

'Nine out of ten local people want the council to reduce the amount of traffic in town,' explains Kylie Challenger, one of the campaign organisers. 'That means banning through traffic from the town centre in the daytime, a better, cheaper bus service and more cycle lanes.'

For more information about N.Y.A.T.F. and its campaign, contact Kylie Challenger or William Powers at Sir Albert Graham School, South Lane, Newtown NT1 6TT.
School telephone no.: 01308 12346.
E-mail:
NAYTF@SirAlbertGraham.sch.co.uk

In groups

Study the press release and the helpful hints (left), then draft a press release about your campaign.

For your file

In groups, discuss what you have learned about how to run a campaign from the information and activities on these pages. Draw up a list of advice – 'Our top ten tips on how to run a campaign'. Then each put a copy of the list in your files, together with a short written statement saying what went well during your campaign, what you've learned from running it and what you would do differently in running another campaign in the future.

What is mental illness?

Mental illness
Some questions and answers

What is mental illness?

Mental illness is the term used to describe an illness that affects the mind rather than the body. Many different types of mental illnesses can affect your mind, just as there are many different physical illnesses which can affect your body.

Mental illnesses often involve feelings of depression, anxiety and confusion. Most people experience such feelings from time-to-time, particularly after a distressing event or during a period of stress. A person suffering from a mental illness experiences these feelings so strongly or over such a long period of time that they find it very hard to cope with everyday life.

What is a nervous breakdown?

Because it can be difficult to describe mental illness exactly, we sometimes say that a person has had a 'nervous breakdown'. We use it to cover a wide range of mental states that make it difficult for a person to cope with life. However, because it doesn't describe a specific mental illness, it's not a term that is used by psychiatrists or psychologists.

How common is mental illness?

Mental illness affects at least 15 people in every 100 at some stage of their lives. So it is likely that at some point you will have a friend or relative that becomes mentally ill.

Can mental illness be cured?

Mental illness is sometimes a temporary condition or one which can be treated successfully, though there is the possibility that it may re-occur. Some mental illnesses can be cured through talking treatments, either individual sessions with a psychiatrist or psychotherapist, or group sessions in which experiences are shared. Other illnesses may require a course of drugs as well.

Are people who are mentally ill dangerous?

A small minority of mentally ill people may become violent and aggressive unless they are treated, but most people are not dangerous. They are far more likely to hurt themselves than other people.

Why are people so afraid of mental illness?

One reason is that people seem to think they will be regarded as weak or strange if they are mentally ill. However, anyone can become mentally ill, it's nothing to be ashamed of.

In groups

1 Sometimes people with mental illnesses are referred to as 'loonies', 'nutters' or 'crackpots'. Some people argue that we should stop using such terms, because by doing so we are discriminating against people who are mentally ill. Others argue that such terms are harmless. What do you think?

2 People who are mentally ill are often the victims of prejudice. Discuss what forms this prejudice takes. Suggest what **a)** individuals, **b)** the media **c)** the government could do to help change people's attitudes.

Mental illness in the family

How can you help someone in your family who is mentally ill? The way you can help most is by accepting that they are ill, giving sympathy and support and ensuring that they get professional help.

Mental health problems

A lot of people find it hard to cope at times. This may be because a friend or relative has died; there may be job worries or money problems; friendships or relationships may have ended unhappily.

When things like this happen, many people naturally feel sad or depressed, alone or angry. Sometimes they may show how they feel by being rude or grumpy, or by wanting to be alone a lot, or to go out all the time. These are usually ordinary reactions to uncomfortable feelings and upsetting events in life that we may all experience.

However, some people's reactions may become more disturbing. For example:

1 Your mother or father refuses to leave her or his room for a long period of time, is unable to make the effort to get washed and dressed, and maybe shouts angrily for most of the day.

2 Your brother or sister thinks that voices are telling him or her what to do and is bewildered and afraid. They could be suffering from a serious mental health problem.

Some types of mental illness

Bipolar disorder (manic depression) causes extreme changes in mood from high spirits and over-activity to deep depression and lethargy; it often causes irritability that can be very wearing for friends and family.

Schizophrenia can lead to a person hearing voices, telling him or her what to do and producing strong feelings of confusion, bewilderment and fear; and it can cause him or her to think that all his or her thoughts are being controlled by others.

There are other types of mental illness, for example, **dementia** in elderly people, when some sufferers may become very forgetful and confused, and their behaviour becomes unpredictable. Some people suffer from **obsessive compulsive disorder** when, for example, they may feel that they have to keep things extremely clean and tidy or they become very anxious.

How does this make you feel?

If your mum or dad or favourite aunt or uncle has become, during this time, a very different person, it may seem that no one is there to look after you, to listen to your worries or problems, or to help you with your feelings, too. You may feel scared, unsure and angry, sad or lonely. You may be ashamed or embarrassed and not understand what is happening. Maybe you don't want anyone else to know. You may even feel angry with them for making you feel so frightened and confused.

It will always help to talk to someone else, and to find an adult who can understand. They may be able to reassure you and help you to get the right support from a doctor or a social worker.

But remember, it is not your responsibility to make them well – there is a limit to how far you can help them. Most people who suffer from periods of mental illness need professional help, arranged through their GP, and they can improve with therapy and medication.

Understanding depression

Depression can mean many different things, because there are different levels of depression. If you are going through a bad patch you may suffer from a mild form of depression. It makes you feel low, but it doesn't stop you from doing everyday things, although everything may seem harder to do and less worthwhile.

A person with severe depression feels a sense of utter hopelessness and that life is so pointless it's not worth doing anything. These feelings are so strong that they make it difficult for the person to cope with life. Their school work may suffer. They may stop wanting to see their friends. They may stop getting up in the morning and keep bursting into tears. They may even contemplate committing suicide.

Symptoms of depression among teenagers

Depressive thoughts among teenagers might focus on their physical shape and size. You may hate the way you look and you may be convinced that you are ugly, or that you can never be loved because of your physical appearance.

You may be preoccupied with negative thoughts and seeing the worst in everything. Rather than feeling alive with anger or grief you are more likely to feel numb, empty and despondent.

Perhaps you feel that you cannot make friends and that you are continually excluded from what is going on around you.

You may wake up early in the mornings and not be able to go back to sleep, or you may sleep for longer than usual. You may find it an effort to do the simplest tasks.

You may feel so awkward and tense when you are with others that the idea of a good relationship with someone you care for seems like an impossible dream.

Work or study may seem a waste of time; you may be convinced that you will never achieve anything and that trying to do your best is therefore pointless.

Don't do it!

One word on running away or suicide – don't. Doing a runner is an admission of defeat – not being able to solve the problem that is causing the depression. Ironically, it would cause far more problems and probably worse ones.

No problem is unsolvable. No problem is so tangled it can't be unwound.

Teenagers have a whole exciting life ahead. You could travel to new places, meet a wonderful partner, try new things, build a home to be happy in, find a fulfilling job – nobody would want to miss all that!

If you or anyone you know shows signs of leaving home or committing suicide, get help at once from a trusted adult.

In groups

What do you learn from this page about the symptoms of depression? How can you tell whether a friend is depressed?

Dealing with depression

How to defeat depression

Depression has two important characteristics you need to be aware of when thinking about what you can do to defeat it:

1. It can feed on itself: you get depressed and then you get more depressed about being depressed.
2. It can occupy enormous amounts of your time and attention.

Being in a state of depression can then itself become a bigger problem than the difficulties which caused it in the first place.

- Find things to do that are so interesting to you that, at least for a while, you forget you are depressed.
- Stop being over-concerned with what goes on 'in your head'. Be physical: walk, run, dance, cycle, play a sport.
- Do anything which will make you laugh.

You need to do things which will make you feel better about yourself.

- Look after yourself physically: do not abuse your body with drugs, eat well and get exercise.
- Pay attention to your appearance and the place you live. Try and make them more how you want them to be.
- Try and take a break from your usual routine.

You need to deal with anything that is wrong in your life. Important principles to bear in mind are:

- Ask for help. Other people can listen and help you think things through.
- Act rather than be passive. Do not let fear stop you from making necessary changes.
- Do not sit on your feelings. If you need to cry, cry. If you need to get angry, get angry.

I'm feeling so depressed

Dear Erica:

I feel so low and depressed all the time over nothing in particular. Things are OK so far as my schoolwork is concerned. I don't have any close friends though – at breaktime I hang around with some other girls in my year, but they're not real mates. I've got a boyfriend but we only see each other every now and then, and we're not that serious. He spends a lot of his time going to football training and he seems more in love with his football than he is with me.

I can't really talk to my mum because she doesn't seem to understand and keeps telling me to snap out of it. And my dad's never there – he's either working or down the pub.

Please tell me why I feel so upset that sometimes all I want to do is cry. I'm beginning to feel desperate.

Nicole

Erica says:

It can be tough when you're growing up. As you go through puberty it's not only that your body changes, your feelings are affected too. Because your hormones are working overtime, it can make you feel moody, depressed and generally dissatisfied. Lots of other teenagers feel the way you do.

There are several things you can do to help yourself feel less depressed. Try to focus on the things that are going well in your life and do something about those that aren't going so well. Don't depend on your boyfriend for your social life. It sounds as if he's got other things on his mind. Arrange to see some of your classmates out of school and get to know some of them better. You could broaden your range of friends by joining some after-school clubs.

As far as your family is concerned, many teenagers feel that their parents don't understand them. If you really can't get through to them about how you're feeling, try talking to another adult you can trust – perhaps a teacher, or another relative, such as a grandparent. Or you could ring a helpline. Talking things through should help you to put things in perspective and see that your life isn't all gloom and doom. Developing a positive attitude will help you feel better.

In groups

Discuss what you learn from this page about what you can do to help you deal with depression.

For your file

Write an article for a teen magazine about depression, its causes and how to deal with it.

Poverty in the UK

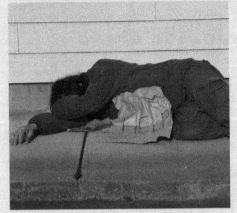

Some people resort to begging to get money to provide their basic needs

What causes poverty?

A number of factors combine to cause poverty and the lack of an adequate income.

Unemployment In 2009 to 2010, 42% of all families which were below the UK poverty line had no member of the family working.

Low paid work Even when people do work, it doesn't necessarily lift them out of poverty. In 2009 to 2010, 58% of families which were below the UK poverty line had one working member. Low wages, part-time work and the high costs of childcare all reduce the effect of being in work.

Inadequate benefits In the UK, when people are out of work or earn insufficient money, the benefits system is designed to offer a safety net. In practice, the benefits are rarely enough to lift the recipient out of poverty.

What is poverty?

Poverty means being so poor that you do not have enough money or material possessions to be able to provide yourself with the basic things you need to survive, such as food, water, clothing and shelter. A person who cannot meet such basic needs is in a condition of **absolute poverty**.

In the past, some of the poorest people in Britain lived in absolute poverty. Today, the welfare state aims to provide benefits that will enable everyone in the UK to meet their basic needs. However, there are still large numbers of people whose standard of living is regarded as below what is acceptable in a modern industrial society. Such people live in **relative poverty** compared to the other members of our society.

In theory, in modern Britain, there are sufficient goods and services to provide everyone with a reasonable standard of living. That poverty continues to exist is not due to a lack of wealth, but rather to how that wealth is distributed.

In groups

"The government should do more to help the poor. Rich people should have to pay more taxes so that benefits for poor people, such as the state pension for older people, could be increased."

Say why you agree or disagree with this view.

Who are the poor?

People are poor for many reasons. But explanations that put poverty down to alcohol and drug dependency, family breakdown, poor parenting or a culture of worklessness are not supported by the facts.

- Families with children are more likely to be poor than those without children and lone parents are more likely to live in poverty than couples.

- Families in which one member is disabled or in which people have to stay at home to care for a person who is sick are more likely to live in poverty.

- Certain ethnic minorities are more likely to live in poverty because of discrimination in the workplace.

- Many older people who have only the state pension and benefits to live off are poor.

In groups

What do you learn from this page about what causes poverty and which groups of people are most likely to be poor?

"The government should do more to help the poor, by providing them with cheap housing and by taxing the rich to pay for higher benefits."

Discuss this view and say what you think should be done to eradicate poverty in the UK.

· Street life ·

Homelessness is growing. And the people sleeping on the streets are only the tip of the iceberg. Emily Moore asks what can be done.

Homelessness

Homelessness means not having a home. You don't have to be living on the street to be homeless – even if you have a roof over your head you can still be without a home. This may be because you don't have any rights to stay where you live or your home is unsuitable for you.

What situations mean you are homeless?

You might be homeless if you are:

- sleeping on the streets
- temporarily staying with friends or family
- having to stay in a hostel or a bed and breakfast hotel
- living in very overcrowded conditions
- at risk of violence or abuse in your home
- living in poor conditions that affect your health
- living in somewhere that you have no right to stay in (e.g. a squat).

Who is affected?

Homelessness affects a wide variety of people. Some groups of people are more likely to become homeless because they have fewer rights, particular needs or are less able to cope by themselves.

These include:

- teenagers who have run away or left home
- old people
- people with physical or mental health problems
- people on benefits or low incomes
- people leaving care
- ex-armed forces personnel
- ex-prisoners
- asylum seekers and refugees.

Street homelessness

The homeless charity Shelter believes the underlying reason in general is lack of affordable housing. People sleeping on the street are the most visible face of homelessness and have the most extreme problems. Street homelessness can be caused by family breakdown, domestic violence, drug or alcohol problems and mental illness. Family breakdown is cited by 38% of homeless people as the key factor that first drove them to sleep rough. According to surveys, only one in five of those who sleep rough do so by choice.

Is there a solution to street homelessness?

There are many problems and many solutions. Long-term solutions include providing more affordable, secure, good-quality housing. But handing someone the key to a council flat is not enough. The street homeless need long-term support, for example with alcohol, drug and mental health problems.

Prevention is better than cure. This means providing more support for vulnerable people *before* they end up on the streets.

In groups

Study the article on homelessness, then discuss these questions.

1. How would you define homelessness?

2. 'Homeless people have only got themselves to blame.' Say why you agree or disagree with this statement. What are the main causes of homelessness?

3. What can be done to solve the problem of homelessness? Draft a letter to the government suggesting what you think it should be doing to reduce homelessness.

For your file

Imagine you are a homeless teenager. What would it be like to live on the street? Think about the dangers you would face, as well as the difficulty of keeping warm and dry and getting enough to eat. Explain how you became homeless and write about what life is like for you.

World poverty – the rich–poor divide

The world can be divided into rich countries, where most of the population have a reasonable standard of living, and poor countries, where large numbers of people live in poverty.

Because the rich countries are highly industrialised, they are often called the developed world. The poor countries are known as less economically developed countries (LEDCs).

The richest 1% of people own 40% of the world's wealth, while 50% of the world's people own only 1% of the world's wealth.

Worlds apart from birth

● One in six children in Sub-Saharan Africa die before the age of 5, compared to one in 143 in the industrialised world.

● Millions of children die each year in poorer countries from preventable causes, because of lack of access to basic services, such as health care, sanitation and clean water.

● A baby born in Bolivia to a mother with no education has a 10% chance of dying, while one born to a woman with at least secondary education has only a 0.4% chance.

Differences between the rich and the poor

The developed world	The less developed world
18% of the world's population	70% of global internet usage
Consumes over 50% of the world's food	18% of people are undernourished
Higher average life expectancy, e.g. 78 years in the UK	Lower average life expectancy, e.g. 46 years in Sub-Saharan Africa
Low infant mortality rate	High death rate for children under 5
Access to education and health care for all	Limited access to education and health care
Low percentage of people living in poverty	High percentage of people living in poverty
Highly industrialised	Limited industrialisation
Well-developed infrastructures, e.g. transport and communications	Less-developed infrastructures
70% of global internet usage	30% of global internet usage

In groups

Discuss the main differences between the rich countries of the developed world and the poor countries that are less economically developed.

For your file

Research using the internet campaigns to end poverty, such as Make Poverty History, and write a letter to a billionaire who is thinking of buying a football club arguing that he should use his money on helping to eliminate poverty instead.

Target likely to be missed

In 2000, the UN set a target of making primary education available to all children in the world by 2015. However, a report in 2008 said the target was likely to be missed.

Although the number of children not in primary education was falling, the report estimated that at least 29 million children will still be out of school in 2015.

Breaking the poverty cycle

Education, especially for girls, empowers families to break the cycle of poverty for good. Young women with a primary education are twice as likely to stay safe from AIDS, and their earnings will be 10–20% higher for every year of schooling completed. Evidence gathered over 30 years shows that educating women is the single most powerful weapon against malnutrition – more effective than improving food supply.

For only $5.4 billion more per year, we could provide a quality, free education to every child, and unlock the full power of education to beat poverty. This amounts to less than 2.5 days' global military spending. For the price of just one of the Cruise missiles dropped on Baghdad, 100 schools could be built in Africa.

For your file

Write a statement explaining why education for all should be at the top of the agenda for governments in less economically developed countries.

scuss what you have learned from this page
out the link between poverty and education.

Education and poverty

Education and poverty are closely related. In many developing countries, people choose to move to cities to find work. However, without a formal education, many of them cannot find a job. This forces them into shanty towns – dwellings on the edge of cities without a clean water supply or proper sanitation. Without an adequate health education, they may not understand the risks of living in such an area.

Poverty also causes a lack of education. Without resources, schools cannot be built, nor teachers paid to teach. Many children do not receive a proper primary or secondary education.

The result is a vicious circle: without education, a country cannot climb out of poverty, but while poverty still exists, education cannot be provided to much of the population.

Assessing your progress and achievements

The aim of this unit is to help you to think about your progress in Year 9, and to discuss it with your tutor, before writing a statement of your achievements. It also gives you the opportunity to review your study habits before you start your GCSE courses.

Preparing your self-assessment

Draft statements expressing your opinion of what you have achieved in Year 9.

1 Write a comment on your **subjects**, saying what progress you think you have made in each one. Give yourself a grade for effort and progress in each subject, and write down your reasons for each grade.

2 Think about the **skills** which you are developing as a result of the work you do in different subjects – communication skills, numeracy skills, study skills, problem-solving skills, personal and social skills, and ICT skills. Comment on how much progress you have made in the development of each of these skills during the past year.

3 List your most significant achievements this year in the **activities** you take part in both inside and out of school. Include details of events organised by clubs and societies that you belong to, sports activities, drama and musical activities and any school events that you have been involved in.

4 Write a comment on what your **behaviour and attitude** have been like in Year 9. Think about you attendance and punctuality; your behaviour in lessons and around the school; how up-to-date you have been with your work; and whether you have volunteered for things and played a full part in the life of the school.

Discussing your progress

Arrange a meeting with your tutor to discuss your self-assessment. Listen carefully to anything your tutor has to say, and add anything they think you have missed out. Note down any comments they make in which they disagree with you, either because they think you have been too harsh on yourself or because they think that you have overestimated your progress.

Setting targets

Use the meeting with your tutor to set targets for Year 10. Identify those subjects and skills that you need to concentrate on improving in Year 10. Discuss what you need to do and the things you will have to change in order to improve those subjects or skills. Then draw up an action plan which lists the steps you are going to take to achieve your goals.

Recording your achievements

Make any alterations to your statements that you think are necessary as a result of your discussion with your tutor and check that your tutor agrees with the changes. Then put your statements in your record of achievement file.

For your file

Draw up a step-by-step action plan for each of the goals that you and your tutor have agreed as your targets for Year 10.

Assessing your study habits

The key to effective studying is good organisation. Before you start your GCSE courses in Year 10, think about how good your study habits are.

Do you plan how to use your time?

Are you good at organising your time so that you can fit in all the things you want to do and still get your schoolwork in on time?

Do you keep a diary or weekly planner?

Do you set aside particular times in the evenings and at weekends to do your homework?

How could you organise the use of your time better in the future?

Have you got a quiet place to study?

You need to find a quiet place to study where you won't be disturbed by other members of your family or by the TV.

If you're finding it hard to study at home, is there a library you could go to, or a room at school which you could use, either before or after school?

Do you keep your files in order?

Do you always put work in the right folder?

Do you regularly spend time sorting out your files, putting papers in order, making sure that they are each dated and numbered?

Do you use dividers so that you can easily find work on different topics?

Do you always put your files back in the same place when you have finished using them?

Are you good at organising how you study?

Do you use your study time as productively as you could? Have you got a routine?

Are you good at prioritising and planning ahead, so that you don't have to do things in a rush before a deadline?

Do you set yourself short-term targets, for example, 'I'll write up the notes and draw the diagram, then I'll have a short break'?

Do you take regular breaks so that your concentration level doesn't drop?

How good are your revision skills?

Do you just spend your time reading and re-reading your notes in the hope that you'll learn them?

Or do you use strategies that will help you to pick out the key facts in a topic, for example by marking them with a highlighter?

Do you make revision cards?

Do you have a 'revision buddy' and take it in turns with your friend to test each other on the facts you are learning?

In pairs

On your own write down what you think are the strengths and weaknesses of your study habits. Then discuss with a partner what each of you could do to improve your study habits.

For your file

Write a statement saying whether or not you think you have good study habits and how you aim to improve them in Year 10.

Acknowledgments

The publishers wish to thank the following for permission to reproduce text. Every effort has been made to trace copyright holders and to obtain their permission for the use of copyright materials. The publishers will gladly receive any information enabling them to rectify any error or omission at the first opportunity.

p7 'Give the right impression – be yourself' extract adapted from *Thirteen Something* by Jane Goldman, published by Piccadilly Press, reprinted with permission of Piccadilly Press; p7 'Four ways to cope with fashion' extract adapted from *Thirteen Something* by Jane Goldman, published by Piccadilly Press, reprinted with permission of Piccadilly Press; p8 'Difficult feelings – anger' from *Wise Guides: Self Esteem* by Anita Naik, published by Hodder & Stoughton, reprinted with permission of Hodder & Stoughton Ltd; p9 'Difficult feelings – frustration' from *Wise Guides: Self Esteem* by Anita Naik, published by Hodder & Stoughton Ltd, reprinted with permission of Hodder & Stoughton Ltd; p10 'What is racism?' extract from *What is racism?* published by Commission for Racial Equality, used with permission; p10 'Racism is…' from 'Stop racism now!' Mizz issue 295 © Mizz/IPC Syndication, reprinted with permission of IPC Syndication; p11 'Racists – what's their problem?' from 'Stop racism now!' *Mizz* issue 295 © Mizz/IPC Syndication, reprinted with permission of IPC Syndication; p11 'Why are some people racist?' extract from *Racism* by Jagdish Gundara and Roger Hewitt, published by Evans Brothers; p12 'Victims of racism' from 'Stop racism now!' *Mizz* issue 295 © Mizz/IPC Syndication, reprinted with permission of IPC Syndication; p13 'How much discrimination is there?' extract from *What is racism?* published by Commission for Racial Equality, used with permission; p13 'Muslims under siege' from *Black Action* October 2008, produced by Unison, reproduced with permission of the National Assembly Against Racism (naar.org.uk) and UNISON (unison.org.uk); p13 quote by John Grieve from 'The evidence against me is compelling…' from *The Daily Telegraph* 10 May 2000 © The Telegraph Group Ltd, used with permission; p14 'Racial attacks and harassment' extract from Racial Attacks and Harassment, produced by the 1990 Trust, used with permission; p15 'Take a stand against racism' extract from *Don't Shut Your Eyes*, produced by Commission for Racial Equality, used with permission; p16 'Do you make your own decisions?' adapted from *Young Citizen Growing Up* by Kate Brooks, published by Wayland, reprinted with permission of Hodder & Stoughton Ltd; p17 'Who influences you?' from *Lifelines 3* published by Collins, adapted from *Active Material Book 3* published by Basil Blackwell; p18 'Consider the consequences' extract from *Introducing Moral Issues* by Joe Jenkins, published by Heinemann Educational, reprinted with permission of REPP; p19 'What is peer pressure?' extract from *Friends and Enemies* by Anita Naik, published by Hodder & Stoughton, reprinted with permission of Hodder & Stoughton; p21 'Educate your parents' extract from *Letter to Growing Pains* by Philip Hodson © Philip Hodson 1988, reprinted with permission of Peters Fraser & Dunlop on behalf of Philip Hodson; p22 'My Bill of Rights' adapted from *Wise Guides: Self Esteem* by Anita Naik, published by Hodder & Stoughton, reprinted with permission of Hodder & Stoughton Ltd; p25 'Human rights activist detained in China' from *Women's rights activist detained in China* Amnesty International 14 January 2009 © Amnesty International Publications; p28 'The right to fight' extract from *Arms and the woman in Europe* by Ian Black, from The Guardian 12 Jan 2000 © *The Guardian*, used with permission; p36 'Can you help a friend in need?' adapted from *It Happened to Me* by Lesley Johnston, published by Macmillan, reprinted with permission of Macmillan; p36 'Someone to talk to' is from 'A helping hand' in *Shout* issue 171 © D.C Thomson & Co. Ltd; p38 'How dangerous is drug taking?' extract from *D-Mag*, used with permission; p39 'Should cannabis be legalised?' extract from *The Big Question: Is it time the world forgot about cannabis in its war on drugs?* by Michael McCarthy from *The Independent* 3 Oct 2008, reprinted with permission; p39 'The benefits of legalisation' from *Should drugs be decriminalised* by Kailash Chand from Student BMJ 16 Feb 2008, reprinted with permission of BMJ Publishing Group; p40 'How to help a friend who has a problem with drugs' extract from *D-Mag*, used with permission; p40 'My life's a mess' from *Drugs – The facts*, reproduced with permission of Health Promotion England; p42 'Why do so many young people commit crimes?' extract from *Introducing Moral Issues* by Joe Jenkins, published by Heinemann Educational, reprinted with permission of REPP; p41 'What to do in an emergency' extract from *D-Mag*, used with permission; p42 'More girls turn to crime' extract from *How children have changed in 50 years* by Celia Hall from *The Telegraph* © Telegraph Group Limited; p43 'Why people do it' from article on shoplifting in *Mizz* issue 253 © Mizz/IPC Syndication; p43 'Rebecca's story' from article in on shoplifting in *Mizz* issue 253 © Mizz/IPC Syndication; p46 'Gang crime and knife crime' from *Gangs and gang crime: the facts* on direct.gov.uk © Crown copyright, reproduced with permission; p46 'I'm being pressured into joining a gang, what can I do?' from *Gangs and gang crime: the facts* on direct.gov.uk © Crown copyright, reproduced with permission; p47 'Have your say – carrying knives' adapted from *Crime and Your Community 4 – Knives and young people*, produced by Crimestoppers; p47 'Cutting down on knife crime' adapted from *Crime and Your Community 4 – Knives and young people*, produced by Crimestoppers; p47 'Don't give in' from safe.met.police.uk, *The Metropolitan Police* © Mayor's Office for Policing and Crime 2014; p51 'Saying what you want – confidence tips' adapted from *Say What You Mean and Get What You Want* by Tricia Kreitman, published by Macmillan, reprinted with permission of Macmillan; p58 'Public interest vs. private rights' adapted from *Viewpoints: Media Power* by Alison Cooper, published 1997 by Franklin Watts of The Watts Published Group Limited, used with permission; p60 'Anorexia nervosa' adapted from *Trouble with eating* by Emily Moore from *The Guardian* 29 October 1996 © The Guardian, used with permission; p60 'Portia's

story' from *Each day is like an abyss* by Christine Doyle from *The Daily Telegraph* 20 June 2000 © Telegraph Group Limited, used with permission; p61 'What causes an eating disorder?' from *Wise Guides: Eating* by Anita Naik, published by Hodder & Stoughton, reprinted with permission of Hodder & Stoughton Ltd; p61 'The red flags of an eating disorder' from *Wise Guides: Eating* by Anita Naik, published by Hodder & Stoughton, reprinted with permission of Hodder & Stoughton Ltd; p61 'Mark's story' extract from *Eating Disorders* by Jenny Bryan, published by Wayland, reprinted with permission of Hodder & Stoughton Ltd; p62 'What is bulimia?' from 'Beating bulimia' in *Shout* issue 144 © D.C. Thomson & Co. Ltd, used with permission; p63 'Is there too much pressure to be thin?' from 'Forced to be thin' from *The Daily Telegraph* 1 July 2000 © Telegraph Group Limited, used with permission; p63 quote by Adele Lovell from *The Just Seventeen Guide to Being Gorgeous*, published by Hodder & Stoughton, reprinted with permission of Hodder & Stoughton Ltd; p72 'What's it like being in custody?' from *Turning my back on crime*, featured on thesite.org; p72 'Mayors' extract from direct.gov.uk © Crown copyright, reproduced with permission; p74 'Political parties and the political spectrum' extract from *You and Your Government* by Graham Skipstone, published by OUP ANZ © Oxford University Press AU, reprinted with permission; p75 'Party policies' from channel4learning.com/lifestuff, reproduced with permission of Channel 4 Learning; p76 'Forming a political party' extract from *You and Your Government* by Graham Skipstone, published by OUP ANZ © Oxford University Press AU, reprinted with permission; p76 'Other political parties' adapted from *Democracy in Action* by Simon Foster, published by Collins, reprinted with permission of HarperCollinsPublishers Ltd; p77 'How would you vote?' extract from *You and Your Government* by Graham Skipstone, published by OUP ANZ © Oxford University Press AU, reprinted with permission; p78 'What is safer sex?' from *14 year olds "regret having had sex"* by Celia Hall from *The Daily Telegraph* 5 May 2000 © Telegraph Group Limited, used with permission; p79 'What to do it you think you have an STI' extract from *Sex: How? Why? What? The Teenager's Guide* by Jane Goldman, published by Piccadilly Press, used with permission of the publishers; p80 'AIDS – The facts' extract from *Sex: How? Why? What? The Teenager's Guide* by Jane Goldman, published by Piccadilly Press, used with permission of Piccadilly Press; p81 'Teenagers think HIV is "irrelevant"' adapted from *Soap gives best AIDS education* from *The Guardian* 1 Dec 1999 © The Guardian, used with permission; p88 'Multinational corporations' from *The A–Z of World Development* by Andy Crump, New Internationalist © New Internationalist Publications, used with permission; p89 extract from 'Supermarkets and sweatshops', reproduced with permission of War on Want; p89 diagram courtesy of Labour Behind the Label, produced under the Creative Commons license creativecommons.org/licenses; p91 'Policing the internet' from *Safe surfing advice*, produced by Childline © NSPCC; p92 'The effects of global warming' adapted from *Global Warming* produced by Young People's Trust for the Environment and Nature Conservation, used with permission; p93 'Slow the global warming' adapted from Global Warming produced by Young People's Trust for the Environment and Nature Conservation, used with permission; p94 'A shattered dream' from *Dreams of peace shattered* by John Gittings from *The Guardian* 27 June 1995 © The Guardian, used with permission; p94 'Why has the UN failed to bring peace?' extract from 'Makkah Imam blasts UN for being a mute spectator' in *Arab News* 12 Aug 2006; p95 'Arms exports' and logo reproduced with permission of CAAT; p95 'Arms exports' quotes from CAAT leaflet, used with permission; p95 'The UK and the arms trade' quotes from Oxfam report *Small Arms, Wrong Hands*, used with permission; p95 'The UK and the arms trade' quotes from World Development Movement leaflet *Conflict and Development*, used with permission; p96 'Pressure group techniques' extract adapted from *Democracy in Action* by Simon Foster, published by Collins, reprinted with permission of HarperCollinsPublishers Ltd; p97 extract from 'It's time to put your feet down', produced by Pedestrians Association, used with permission; p99 'Hitting the headlines' adapted from *Causing a stink! The Eco Warrior's Handbook* by Caroline Layton, published by Bloomsbury, reprinted with permission of Friends of the Earth; p99 'How to write a good press release' adapted from *Causing a stink! The Eco Warrior's Handbook* by Caroline Layton, p99 'Press Release' adapted from *Causing a stink! The Eco Warrior's Handbook* by Caroline Layton, published by Bloomsbury, reprinted with permission of Friends of the Earth; p101 'Mental health problems' extract from *Mental Health Problems – What Do They Mean?* published by Young Minds, used with permission; p102 'Symptoms of depression among teenagers' from Understanding Depression, produced by MIND (National Association for Mental Health) © MIND 2000, used with permission; p103 'How to defeat depression' from Understanding Depression, produced by MIND (National Association for Mental Health) © MIND 2000, used with permission; p105 'Homelessness' from *What is homelessness?* from shelter.org.uk, reproduced with permission of Shelter; p105 'Is there a solution to street homelessness?' from article by Emily Moore in *The Guardian* 23 Nov 1999 © The Guardian, used with permission; p106 'Worlds apart from birth' from Childmatters newsletter Winter 99/Spring 00, reprinted with permission of the UK Committee for UNICEF; p107 'Breaking the poverty cycle' adapted from *School report 2005 – Rich Countries*, produced by Global Campaign for Education, reproduced with permission; p107 'Education and poverty' adapted from *Global Concerns* by Simon Foster, published by Collins, reprinted with permission of HarperCollinsPublishers Ltd.